THE
SERMON
ON THE
MOUNT

THE
SERMON
ON THE
MOUNT

CONTEMPORARY INSIGHTS
FOR A CHRISTIAN LIFESTYLE

J. DWIGHT PENTECOST

MULTNOMAH PRESS
PORTLAND, OREGON 97266

Other books by J. Dwight Pentecost:

The Glory of God
Things to Come
The Joy of Fellowship
The Joy of Living
Things Which Become Sound Doctrine
Your Adversary the Devil
Design for Discipleship
Prophecy for Today

Cover design by Britt Taylor Collins

Second Edition

First Printing, 1980

Library of Congress Cataloging Publication Data

Pentecost, J. Dwight
    The Sermon on the mount.

    First ed. published in 1975 under title: Design for living.
    Includes indexes.
    1. Sermon on the mount. I. Title.
BT380.2.P37   1980   226'.907   80-13167
ISBN 0-930014-40-5 (pbk.)

Printed in the United States of America

To
my sons in the faith
who share in the
ministry of the Word.

Contents

Introduction

How does one interpret the Sermon on the Mount? Jesus Christ spoke of the righteous requirments revealed in the Old Testament Law, requirements needed for one to enter into the kingdom. Yet He gave this sermon as an example of the kind of life which His followers were to lead by faith. How Christ related the Law to the life of faith must be understood before one can interpret the Sermon on the Mount—before one can see how it applies to his life today. But first we must look at the context in which this, the most famous of sermons, is found—the Gospel of Matthew.

Matthew's Gospel was written to demonstrate to the nation Israel that Jesus Christ was Israel's promised and covenanted Messiah, and to explain to Israel why, since He was the true Messiah, His kingdom was not established at His coming. The first and second chapters of the Gospel demonstrate Christ's legal right to the throne and His recognition by Gentiles (the wise men) as the Messiah.

In the third chapter, John the Baptist appears as a morning star in the darkness of Israel's night to proclaim a message to Israel, "Repent ye: for the kingdom of heaven is at hand" (3:2). John announced that the kingdom God had promised to David in 2 Samuel 7:16 was near at hand. With these words John introduced the Messiah to the nation that had long awaited His coming.

Multitudes accepted John's message in faith and joined themselves together by submitting to John's baptism to await Messiah's coming, expecting to receive from Him the forgiveness of sins. Jesus Christ presented Himself to John to receive John's baptism so that He might fulfill all prophecy, that He might identify Himself with John's

5

6

message. He was baptized to identify Himself with a believing remnant in the nation Israel. It was at his baptism that God authenticated both the person and the work of Jesus Christ.

In the fourth chapter, Matthew shows Christ's moral right to be Israel's king through His triumph over Satan and the temptations in the wilderness.

The time had now come for Christ to begin His ministry, and Christ's first spoken word to the nation Israel was, "Repent: for the kingdom of heaven is at hand" (4:17). In order to authenticate His person and His offer of the covenanted kingdom to Israel, "Jesus went about all Galilee, teaching in their synagogues, and preaching the gospel of the kingdom, and healing all manner of sickness and all manner of disease among the people" (4:23). As a result, great multitudes of people from Galilee and from Decapolis and from Jerusalem and from Judea and from beyond Jordan followed Him (4:25). Those who pressed on our Lord would have been those who heard John's message, were convinced of the need of righteousness, were awaiting the establishment of Messiah's kingdom, and would have been called Jesus' disciples by virtue of the fact that they were willing to be taught by Him.

This multitude came together to learn from the King the conditions upon which they would be admitted to His kingdom. The Old Testament had made it very clear that only the righteous would be accepted into Messiah's kingdom. In Psalm 24 in response to the question, "Who shall ascend into the hill of the Lord? or who shall stand in his holy place?" the answer is given, "He that hath clean hands, and a pure heart; who hath not lifted up his soul unto vanity, nor sworn deceitfully" (24:3-4). The prophet Zechariah in chapters 12 and 13 had made it clear that apart from confession of sin and the reception of cleansing for sin there could be no entrance into Messiah's kingdom. In Ezekiel 36:26-27, God had promised that He would give them a new heart and a new spirit and would cause them to walk in His statutes. Unless they had been saved from their uncleanness, they could not share the glory of Messiah's kingdom.

Righteousness, then, was a prerequisite to entrance into the kingdom. This company knew nothing but the righteousness as defined by the Pharisees. According to their teaching, the observance of the tradition of men would make all of Abraham's physical descendants eligible for entrance into Messiah's kingdom. *The question the multitude had before them was the question as to whether the righteousness of the Pharisees was sufficient for entrance into the kingdom.* It is this important question to which our Lord addressed Himself as He gathered the multitudes unto Him and opened His mouth to teach them.

Our Lord on this occasion did what He so frequently did when discussing the question of righteousness. He turned to the Law. This brings us to another question: *What is the purpose of the Law?*

Such is the question the Apostle Paul faced with his readers in the third chapter of Galatians as he taught them the doctrine of sanctification by faith in Jesus Christ. Paul is dealing with the problem as to how a person is sanctified (made perfect) or how he attains experientially the promises and blessings that are his in Christ. The Galatians had been led to believe that sanctification is by the Law; through the keeping of the Law, believers obtain the promises that were given to them by God. In order to show the fallacy of this interpretation, the apostle has cited the experience of Abraham. Abraham was given promises by God (Gen 12) which were repeated (Gen 13) and ratified by a blood covenant (Gen 15). All that Abraham obtained he obtained by faith since no Law had been given in Abraham's time. Therefore, all that Abraham realized, he had to realize by faith in the promise of God.

The error that had been propagated among the Galatians was that although Abraham attained the promises of God by faith alone, the giving of the Law altered the basic plan by which God dealt with men. Therefore, Abraham's children subsequent to the giving of the Law must attain by keeping the Law rather than by faith in the promise of God. In order to dispel this error, Paul shows in verse 17 of the third chapter of Galatians that "the law, which was four hundred and thirty years after, cannot disannul, that it should make the promise of none effect." Paul adds in verse 19 that rather than disallowing the Law or nullifying the Law, the Law was added, or, better, added alongside, the existing promise, in order to serve a specific function. He further shows in verse 21 that there is no basic conflict between the Law and the promises of God and that the two can coexist. Anticipating certain objections or questions in the minds of his readers, Paul faces the question specifically. "Wherefore, then, serveth the law?" (v. 19). It is this specific question that must be considered now.

It should be observed that many who lived under the Law had the deepest reverence, respect, and love for the Law. David writing in Psalm 119 frequently reflects this attitude. In verse 97 he says, "O how I love thy law! It is my meditation all the day." Or in verse 77 he adds, "Thy law is my delight." Again in verses 103-104, he wrote, "How sweet are thy words unto my taste! yea, sweeter than honey to my mouth! Through thy precepts I get understanding." Or once again, in verse 159, he said, "Consider how I love thy precepts." David shows a love for and a dependence upon the Law. In contrast with much current teaching which treats the Law as a worthless, worn-out garment to be discarded, the Apostle Paul in Romans 7:12 says, "The law is holy, and the commandment holy, and just, and good." That which is loved, revered, and respected by Old and New Testament writers must be served a worthy function.

It needs to be noted that the Law of Moses was given to a redeemed people. The writer to the Hebrews in Hebrews 11:28-29, says of Moses, "Through faith he kept the passover, and the sprinkling of blood, lest he that destroyed the firstborn should touch them. By faith they passed through the Red Sea as by dry land." Israel, the night of the Passover in Egypt, was redeemed by blood. By faith they began a walk through the wilderness toward the land of promise.

It was on the basis of that blood redemption that God could say to the nation as recorded in Isaiah 43:1, "But now thus saith the Lord that created thee, O Jacob, and he that formed thee, O Israel, Fear not: for I have redeemed thee, I have called thee by thy name; thou art mine." The nation that was redeemed by faith through blood was brought to Mount Sinai. *Although that nation had been redeemed, it was a nation which was viewed as being in spiritual immaturity.* They recognized a responsibility to the Redeemer which they did not know how to discharge.

The fact of Israel's infancy at the time of the giving of the Law is recognized by the Apostle Paul who writes in Galatians 3:23-26,

> But before faith came, we were kept under the law, shut up unto the faith which should afterwards be revealed. Wherefore the law was our schoolmaster to bring us unto Christ, that we might be justified by faith. But after that faith is come, we are no longer under a schoolmaster. For ye are all the children of God by faith in Christ Jesus.

Or again in Galatians 4:1-5,

> Now I say, That the heir, as long as he is a child, differeth nothing from a servant, though he be lord of all; but is under tutors and governors until the time appointed of the father. Even so we, when we were children, were in bondage under the elements of the world: but when the fulness of the time was come, God sent forth his Son, made of a woman, made under the law, to redeem them that were under the law, that we might receive the adoption of sons.

Paul views those living under the Law as children in a state of immaturity, and he views the Law *as a pedagogue, a child trainer or overseer whose responsibility it was to supervise every area of the life of the child committed to its care.* It is because of this fact of immaturity that Israel needed the Law. Thus the Law was given as a gracious provision by God to a redeemed, but spiritually immature people to meet their needs.

As the Scriptures are studied, a number of reasons may be derived why the Mosaic Law was given to the nation Israel. *First, it was given to reveal the holiness of God.* Peter writes in I Peter 1:15-16, "But as he which hath called you is holy, so be ye holy in all manner of conversation; because it is written, Be ye holy; for I am holy." The fact that God was a holy God was made very clear to Israel in the Law of Moses. Perhaps the primary function of the Law was to reveal to the people of Israel the fact of the holiness of God and to make them aware of the character of the God who had redeemed them from Egypt. All the requirements laid upon the nation Israel were in the light in the holy character of God as revealed in the Mosaic Law.

Second, the Mosaic Law was given to reveal or expose the sinfulness of man. It is of this that Paul writes in Galatians 3:19b,22, when he says, "It (the Law) was added because of transgressions, till the seed should come to whom the promise was made; and it was ordained by angels in the hand of a mediator. ... But the Scripture hath concluded all under sin, that the promise by faith of Jesus Christ might be given to them that believe."

The holiness of God as revealed in the Law became the test of man's thoughts, words, and actions, and anything that failed to conform to the revealed holiness of God was sin. It is this fact that Paul has in mind when he writes in Romans 3:23, "For all have sinned, and come short of the glory of God." That in which God finds His highest glory is His own holiness. Sin is not only want of conformity unto the Law but want of conformity unto the holiness of God of which the Law is a revelation.

Consequently the holiness of God becomes the final test of sin rather than the Law which is the reflection of that holiness. Because all Abraham's seed were born in sin, the Law was given by which the people of Israel might readily determine their sinfulness before a Holy God. The Law made very specific the requirements of divine holiness so that even children in spiritual infancy could determine whether their conduct was acceptable to a holy God.

A third purpose of the Law, related to the above, was to reveal the standard of holiness required of those in fellowship with a holy God. Israel had been redeemed as a nation. They were redeemed in order to enjoy fellowship with God. As these redeemed ones faced the question of what kind of life was required of those who walk in fellowship with their Redeemer, the Law was given to reveal the standard that God required. It is this the psalmist recognized in Psalm 24:3-5 as he said,

> Who shall ascend into the hill of the Lord? or who shall stand in his holy place? He that hath clean hands, and a pure heart; who hath not lifted up his soul unto vanity, nor sworn deceitfully. He shall receive the blessing from the Lord, and righteousness from the God of his salvation.

Those who were redeemed were redeemed to enjoy the Redeemer, and the Law made it very clear the kind of life that was required if they were to walk in fellowship with Him.

A fourth purpose of the Law is stated by the apostle in Galatians 3:24, "Wherefore the law was our schoolmaster ... unto Christ." The word schoolmaster refers to the slave selected by the father whose responsibility it was to supervise the total development of the child—physically, intellectually, and spiritually. The child was under the pedagogue's constant supervision till such time he should move out of infancy into adulthood. Every area of the child's life was under the supervision of the pedagogue until he came to maturity. *It is the teaching of the apostle that the Law served to supervise physical, mental, and spiritual development of the redeemed Israelite until he should come to maturity in Christ.* The psalmist reflects this same concept in Psalm 119:71-72, "It is good for me that I have been afflicted; that I might learn thy statutes. The law of thy mouth is better unto me than thousands of gold and silver." David confesses that through the Law he learned of God's requirements.

A fifth purpose of the Law is that it was given to be the unifying principle that made possible the establishment of the nation. In Exodus 19:5-8 one reads,

> Now therefore, if ye will obey my voice indeed, and keep my covenant, then ye shall be a peculiar treasure unto me above all people: for all the earth is mine: and ye shall be unto me a kingdom of priests, and an holy nation. These are the words which thou shalt speak unto the children of Israel. And Moses came and called for the elders of the people, and laid before their faces all these words which the Lord commanded him. And all the people answered together, and said, All that the Lord hath spoken we will do.

One notices in the eighth verse that in response to the instruction given by Moses as to what God had revealed, the nation voluntarily submitted themselves to the authority of the Law. Apart from the voluntary submission to a unifying principle there could have been no nation. And the people redeemed out of Egypt by blood who had begun a walk by faith were constituted a nation when they voluntarily submitted themselves unto the Law.

This same truth is reaffirmed in Deuteronomy 5:27-28,

> "Go thou near, and hear all that the Lord our God shall say: and speak thou unto us all that the Lord our God shall speak unto thee; and we will hear it, and do it. And the Lord heard the voice of your words, when ye spake unto me; and the Lord said unto me, I have heard the voice of the words of this people, which they have spoken unto thee: they have well said all that they have spoken."

From the divine viewpoint Israel was constituted a nation at the time the people voluntarily submitted themselves unto the Law.

It is significant that the prophet Jeremiah warns the people that because they have abandoned the Law, God will deliver them into the hand of the Gentiles. The Babylonian captivity by which Israel lost her national identity came about because of the peoples' failure to observe the Law. In Deuteronomy 28 Moses had made it very clear that if the people abandoned the Law, God would deliver them into the hands of the Gentiles. And it is not without significance that until Israel submits to the authority of the law of her Messiah-King, she will not be recognized by God as a nation again.

A sixth purpose somewhat related to the above is that the Law was given to Israel to separate Israel from the nations in order that they might become a kingdom of priests. In Exodus 31:13 one reads "Speak thou also unto the children of Israel, saying, Verily my sabbaths ye shall keep: for it is a sign between me and you throughout your generations; that ye may know that I am the Lord that doth sanctify you." Israel was sanctified or set apart, according to Exodus 19:5,6, to become a kingdom of priests, that is, a nation that mediated the truth of God to the nations of the earth. The Law became a hedge that separated Israel from the nations of the earth. The Law separated, preserved, and kept the nation intact. In order that Israel might serve the function of a light to the world, the people were given the Law, that the Law might separate them from the nations.

In the seventh place, the Law was given to a redeemed people to make provision for forgiveness of sins and restoration to fellowship. In Leviticus 1-7 there are the five offerings that God instituted for the nation. While the nation as a nation was preserved before God because of the annual offering of the blood of atonement, individuals in the nation were restored to fellowship and received forgiveness for specific sins through the use of the offerings that God provided. The God who had redeemed the nation by faith through blood provided that the redeemed could walk in fellowship with Himself. The same Law that revealed their unworthiness for fellowship also provided for restoration to the fellowship. This was one of the primary functions of the Law.

In the eighth place, the Law was given to make provision for a redeemed people to worship. A redeemed people will be a worshipping people, and a people who walk in fellowship with God will worship the God with whom they enjoy fellowship. In Leviticus 23 the Law revealed a cycle of feasts which the nation was expected to observe annually. These feasts were the means by which the nation as a redeemed nation worshipped God. In the cycle of feasts, Israel's attention was directed backward to the redemption out of Egypt and forward to the final redemption that would be provided through the Redeemer according to God's promise.

The Law, in the ninth place, provided a test as to whether one was in the kingdom or the theocracy over which God ruled. In Deuteronomy 28, as Israel stood on the border of the promised land, Moses revealed the principle by which God would deal with the nation. The first portion of the chapter outlines the blessings that would come upon the nation for obedience. A great portion of that extensive chapter deals with the curses that would come on the nation because of disobedience. Even though the nation as a whole entered into the promised land, because not all believed God, not all were eligible to receive the blessings promised to those in the land. The Law, then, became that which revealed whether or not a man was rightly related to God. Those who submitted to and obeyed the Law did so because of their faith in God which produced obedience. Those who disobeyed the Law did so because they were without faith in God, and lack of faith produced their disobedience. Whether or not a man obeyed the Law, then, became the test as to whether he was rightly related to God or in God's kingdom.

Finally, it becomes clear from the New Testament that the Law was given to reveal Jesus Christ. The great truths concerning the person and the work of the Lord Jesus Christ are woven throughout the Law, and the Law was given in order that it might prepare the nation for the coming Redeemer King. It was because of this that the Lord on the Emmaus road could expound to His companions great truths concerning the Messiah that had been revealed in the Law and the Prophets. Israel, through the Law, was being prepared for the coming

Messiah through the revelation of Him which it contained.

As one looks back over these reasons for the giving of the Law, he can observe that there was in the Law that which was revelatory of the holiness of God. This aspect of the Law was permanent. Holiness does not change from age to age, and that which revealed the holiness of God to Israel may still be used to reveal the holiness of God to men today. That which reveals the holiness of God reveals concomitantly the unholiness of men today. It is this revelatory aspect of the Law that Paul refers to as holy, just, and good.

There was also that in the Law which was regulatory. The Law regulated the life and the worship of the Israelite. It is this regulatory aspect of the Law that was temporary, that has been done away. Paul in 1 Timothy 1:8 writes, "But we know that the law is good, if a man use it lawfully."

How can the Law be used lawfully in an age in which it is said that the Law has been done away? If a Law is used to reveal the holiness of God, the unholiness of man, the requirements of those who would live in fellowship with the holy God, or to learn of the person and work of Christ, it is used lawfully. One who attempts to use the regulatory portions of the Law which were "only until Christ" is using the Law unlawfully. While one sings, "Free from the law, O happy condition," one still recognizes that the Law is "Holy, just, and good."

Christ in the Sermon on the Mount uses the Law lawfully to reveal the holiness of God and the demands that the holiness of God makes upon those who would walk in fellowship with Him. Christ discusses first the subjects of the kingdom (5:1-16), describing their character (vv. 1-12) and their influence (vv. 13-16).

The major portion of the Sermon on the Mount shows the relationship of the King to the Mosaic Law (5:17-7:6). In this portion Christ reveals Himself as the One who fulfills the Law (5:17-20). He then proceeds (5:21-48) to reject the Pharisaic traditional interpretation of the Law.

He rejects their interpretation of the Law of murder (21-26), of adultery (27-30), of divorce (31-32), of oaths (33-37), of retaliation (38-42), and finally of love (43-48). He rejects their tradition, not because they did not know the Law, for it is accurately quoted, but He rejected their interpretation of the Law, for they taught that God was concerned only with external actions and not the internal attitudes.

Christ next rejects the Pharisaic practice of the Law (6:1-7:6). He rejects their practice of alms giving (6:1-4), of prayer (6:5-15), and of fasting (6:16-18). He rejects their attitude toward wealth (6:19-24). He rejects their practice of faith (6:25-34) and rejects their practice of judging (7:1-6). Our Lord concludes the sermon by giving instruction to those who would enter the kingdom (7:7-27). He teaches them concerning prayer (vv. 7-11) and true righteousness (v. 12). He shows them the way of access into the kingdom through faith in His words (vv. 13-14). He warns them against the false teachers who sought to lead them astray (vv. 15-23) and offers them a true foundation upon which to build (vv. 24-29).

Thus the Lord, in rejecting both the Pharisaic interpretation of the Law and the Pharisaic practice of the Law, brought this multitude to the conclusion "That except your righteousness shall exceed the righteousness of the scribes and Pharisees, ye shall in no case enter into the kingdom of heaven" (5:20). He closed by offering Himself as the narrow way and as the solid foundation through whom they could come into the kingdom and upon which they could stand. The sermon was designed to lead this multitude away from a false concept of righteousness to a true concept of righteousness, from a false hope of entrance into the kingdom to a sure foundation for entrance into Messiah's kingdom.

While we recognize that the Sermon on the Mount in its historical setting was Christ's instruction to the generation to which He was offering Himself as Saviour and Sovereign, we realize that it has a present-day application. The holiness of God does not change from age to age. The demands of God's holiness do not alter from day to day. When the Sermon on the Mount is viewed as revealing the holiness of God, it becomes a guide as to demands that God's holiness makes upon believers today.

In no sense is the sermon a means of attaining right-eousness; instead, it is a revelation of the righteousness of God and reflects the demands that the holiness of God makes upon those who would walk in fellowship with Him. In the following chapters, we propose to show how this sermon of Christ affects the conduct of those who would walk with God and thus how we can "use the Law lawfully."

1

The Poor in Spirit

Matthew 5:1-12

Many who had seen the miracles that the Lord Jesus performed were persuaded He was actually the King God had promised, who would institute a reign over the nation Israel. They pressed upon Him with one question uppermost, "Are we righteous enough to enter His Kingdom?" They knew well that the Old Testament demanded righteousness as the basis of acceptance with God; and they knew well the declaration of the psalmist that only those with clean hands and a pure heart could stand in the King's presence. And they came to inquire of Him concerning the righteousness He required for entrance into His Kingdom.

Our Lord shocked the multitude, who were devotees of the Pharisees and who zealously pursued Pharisaic righteousness, when He said, "Except your righteousness shall exceed the righteousness of the scribes and Pharisees, ye shall in no case enter into the kingdom of heaven" (5:20). If Pharisaic righteousness, which required a rigid observance of 365 prohibitions and 250 commandments, was not sufficient to bring men into Messiah's Kingdom, what kind of righteousness was necessary?

The Sermon on the Mount was our Lord's exposition of the holiness of God, and the demands that a holy God made. It describes the kind of righteousness that God expects of those who have come to know Him by faith. In that well-known, well-loved, and oft-quoted—but little

19

understood—part of the Sermon we call the Beatitudes, our Lord described the characteristics of a righteous man and laid the foundation of a happy life. He showed what will characterize one who has been made righteous by faith in God's promise. He also gave us the basis upon which God's blessing comes upon those who have received Him as a personal Saviour. We could well call the Beatitudes, "The Basis of a Happy Life."

The Lord's first beatitude is Matthew 5:3: "Blessed are the poor in spirit: for theirs is the kingdom of heaven." God alone is the blessed One. He is worthy to receive blessing because of His absolute, unalterable holiness. One who has been blessed of God is indeed happy, and the word translated "blessed" in this passage of Scripture might best be translated "happy." God alone is worthy to be called blessed because of what He is in His intrinsic character; but God can bestow blessings upon a man. The one who receives God's blessings is a truly happy man.

This word is used frequently in the New Testament to describe the condition of those whom God blesses. In John 13:17 the Lord, at the conclusion of the first of the great lessons to the disciples in the upper room just before His death, turned and said, "If ye know these things, happy are ye if ye do them." The same word translated "blessed" in Matthew 5 is translated here as "happy." Our Lord said that the happiness of the disciples would depend not only on knowing the truth, but also on believing and obeying it.

In John 20:29 the same word is used as our Lord said to Thomas, "Because thou hast seen me, thou hast believed: blessed are they that have not seen, and yet have believed." He who believes will be a truly happy man.

Paul used the same word in 1 Timothy 1:11, "According to the glorious gospel of the blessed God, which was committed to my trust." He wrote here of the contentment that belongs to God because of who God is. Unhappiness is not found in God. Because He is a happy God, He confers His happiness upon those who believe Him.

Then again in Titus 2:13, the apostle, speaking of the coming of Christ, said we are "looking for that blessed hope, and the glorious appearing of the great God and our Saviour Jesus Christ." It is a hope that brings happiness to the believer. The words translated "blessed" would be better translated by our English word *happy*, for they speak of that bestowed by a blessed God; the result is a happy, content, satisfied people.

The word *happy*, as used among the Greeks, originally described the condition of the Greek gods who were deemed to be satisfied, or content, because they had everything they desired and were free to enjoy everything they possessed without restriction. To the Greek mind, happiness had to do with material possessions and the freedom to enjoy them. Their happiness had to do with unrestrained, unlimited gratification of physical desires. Since no limits were ever put upon their deities, the Greeks deemed the gods to be happy. When they lived with the same liberty they ascribed to their gods, they deemed themselves a happy people. Happiness for the Greeks was related to the physical and material world.

But when our Lord spoke of happiness, He related it to holiness. Such is the biblical concept, for in the New Testament, happiness is identified with purity of character. The Word sees sin as the fountainhead of misery, and holiness as the source of peace, satisfaction, and contentment—all that we include in our word *happy*. So, when the Lord said, "Blessed are the poor in spirit," He gave the first characteristic of holiness that produces happiness, so as to lay the foundation for a godly, happy life.

The Lord showed what must characterize a man who says he is holy, and the blessing that comes from God upon one who has received His gift of righteousness by faith in Christ. How significant that the very characteristic the world despises, discounts, and calls a sign of weakness, our Lord exalted. The world can never provide the foundation for a happy life, for the world cannot produce holiness—and there is no happiness apart from holiness.

The word "poor," which the Lord used in Matthew 5:3, is a very interesting and graphic word. To understand its usage, turn to Luke 16:19-22:

> There was a certain rich man, which was clothed in purple
> and fine linen, and fared sumptuously every day: and there
> was a certain beggar named Lazarus, which was laid at his
> gate, full of sores, and desiring to be fed with the crumbs
> which fell from the rich man's table: moreover the dogs
> came and licked his sores. And it came to pass, that the
> beggar died, and was carried by the angels into Abraham's
> bosom.

The word translated "beggar" (vv. 20, 22) is the identical word translated "poor" in Matthew 5:3. The beggar was destitute, poverty-stricken, without any resources whatsoever. The words *poor* and *beggar* come from a root word which means "to cover" or "to cringe." It so humiliated a man to confess he had nothing and was dependent on someone else that the very act of begging demeaned him. So the beggar would cover his face and crouch, or cower, as he held out his hand for an alm. He was ashamed to let the giver know his identity.

Our Lord did not choose this word lightly when He said, "Blessed are the beggars in spirit, blessed are the spiritual paupers, blessed are the spiritually destitute, blessed are the spiritually bankrupt ones who cringe and cower because of their helplessness; for theirs is the kingdom of heaven." In spiritual things, poor in spirit is the opposite not of self-esteem but of spiritual pride. It is the self-sufficiency that springs from spiritual pride that our Lord condemned.

The New Testament records that the Pharisees were intensely proud, for they counted themselves as righteous; they deemed themselves to be righteous and to need nothing. They heard the Lord Jesus offer a true righteousness from God, and they spurned it. This word is addressed to them and to those who follow their path. The man who is characterized by spiritual pride will receive nothing from God; there can be no blessing of God upon him, for pride is no foundation for righteousness. Spiritual pride is not an evidence of holiness but of sinfulness. Spiritual pride can never produce happiness. "Blessed are the spiritual paupers, for theirs is the kingdom of heaven."

The poor in spirit is the one from whom the ground of self-sufficiency has been taken. The poor in spirit is the heart on its knees. The poor in spirit is the one characterized by an attitude of utter dependence. In this instance, as in all the Beatitudes, the Lord did not institute a new concept. Rather, He went back into the Old Testament, particularly the psalms, and gathered together what Scripture had so clearly taught before so that He, from Scripture, might describe righteousness and holiness and the basis of a blessed, happy life.

The psalmist wrote: "The sacrifices of God are a broken spirit: a broken and a contrite heart, O God, thou wilt not despise" (Ps 51:17). Again in Psalm 34:18: "The LORD is nigh unto them that are of a broken heart; and saveth such as be of a contrite spirit." When the psalmist referred to a broken, contrite heart, he did not mean a heart crushed because of bereavement, but a heart that has come to the end of itself, which sees no help in itself, and cries out to God for deliverance.

When the Lord said, "Blessed are the poor in spirit," He spoke to His hearers first of all concerning the way of access to Himself. This is so graphically illustrated in Luke 18:9-14:

> He spake this parable unto certain which trusted in themselves that they were righteous, and despised others: Two men went up into the temple to pray; the one a Pharisee, and the other a publican [tax collector]. The Pharisee stood and prayed thus with himself, God, I thank thee, that I am not as other men are, extortioners, unjust, adulterers, or even as this publican. I fast twice in the week, I give tithes of all that I possess. And the publican, standing afar off, would not lift up so much as his eyes unto heaven, but smote upon his breast, saying, God be merciful to me a sinner. I tell you, this man went down to his house justified rather than the other: for every one that exalteth himself shall be abased; and he that humbleth himself shall be exalted.

The Lord, in such a graphic lesson, presented the truth He stated when He said, "Blessed are the poor in spirit."

This Pharisee stood in a public place to commend himself to God because of what he was: "I am not as other men, extortioners, unjust, adulterers, or as this tax collector." He was controlled by pride and commended himself to God and demanded that God accept him and his petition because of what he was. Then he commended himself to God because of what he had done: "I fast twice in the week, I give tithes of all that I possess." He expected to be blessed of God because of what he had done for God. What an example of the one with no poverty of spirit!

On the other hand, there cowered afar off a confessed sinner who cried, "God, be merciful to me a sinner." "God, look upon me as you look upon the mercy seat sprinkled with atoning blood." This one claimed nothing as to his person nor as to his righteousnesses. In his spiritual poverty and destitution he cast himself wholely upon the grace and mercy of God. Here was a man poor in spirit, and our Lord said, "I tell you, this man went down to his house justified rather than the other: for every one that exalteth himself shall be abased; and he that humbleth himself [is poor in spirit] shall be exalted" (18:14). A man's only way of access to God is to come to God and confess his own unrighteousness, his own inability to meet the standards and requirements of God, and by faith claim the blood of Christ, which covers his sin. As Toplady's words in "Rock of Ages" express it, "Nothing in my hand I bring, simply to Thy cross I cling." Such a one—poor in spirit—is happy because he is blessed of God.

But our Lord not only showed the way of access to Himself, and the way of access into His kingdom, but also He showed what will characterize one who in poverty of spirit has come to claim God's salvation. His life as a child of God will be marked by that same complete dependence upon God, moment by moment.

Paul, in Philippians 3:3, evidenced this poverty of spirit when he said "We . . . have no confidence in the flesh." Again, he wrote in Romans 8:4-5, "That the righteousness of the law might be fulfilled in us, who walk not after the flesh, but after the Spirit. For they that are after the flesh do mind the things of the flesh; but they that are after the Spirit the things of the Spirit." The man who by the flesh seeks to please God claims he can do it himself. In pride he seeks to please God. The only one who pleases God in his daily life is the one who says, "God, I can't do it because the flesh is corrupt; but I cast myself totally and completely upon the sustaining strength of the Holy Spirit that he might live the life of Christ through me."

When Peter stepped out of the boat to walk across the water to the Lord Jesus and began to sink, he cried out, "Lord, help me." He was poor in spirit. When Mary and Martha were overcome with grief at the passing of their brother Lazarus and they sent a message to Jesus Christ to come and help them, they evidenced they were beggars in spirit. When you recognize your own helplessness and cast yourself solely upon the grace of God and the Spirit of God, you are renouncing spiritual pride and evidencing a poverty of spirit that makes it possible for God to bestow blessing after blessing on your life.

What do you have to offer God? Nothing. What does God have to give you? Everything. What makes God's riches yours? A cry for help, a cry of dependence, a confession of your own helplessness. "Blessed are the poor in spirit: for their's is the kingdom of heaven."

2

Comfort in Tears

Matthew 5:4

Our lot is cast in a vale of tears, and there is much in the experience of the child of God day after day to bring tears to the eyes. Yet our Lord has promised, "Blessed are they that mourn: for they shall be comforted." As we turn to the pages of the Word we find frequent reference to those upon whom the burdens of life press so heavily that they give way to tears.

There are tears of bereavement. In the eleventh chapter of John's gospel, Lazarus was taken from the home circle in Bethany by death. Mary and Martha were bereft of their beloved brother. On His way to the grave, Jesus was met by the weeping Mary and the other mourners. He was deeply moved and wept also.

In Psalm 42:1-3, we hear the cry of the psalmist's heart: "As the hart panteth after the water brooks, so panteth my soul after thee, O God. My soul thirsteth for God, for the living God: when shall I come and appear before God? My tears have been my meat day and night, while they continually say unto me, Where is thy God?" The psalmist was reduced to tears because of his utter loneliness. Forsaken by men, pursued by adversaries, he cried out to God in his loneliness because he had been abandoned.

In 2 Timothy 1:3-4, Paul wrote to his son in the faith, Timothy: "I thank God, whom I serve from my forefathers with pure conscience, that without ceasing I have remembrance of thee in my prayers night and day; greatly desiring to see thee, being mindful of thy tears, that I may be filled with joy." In 2 Timothy, we find Timothy's tears coursing down his cheeks because of defeat and discouragement. Here was a man who had been faithful in the ministry, preaching the Word of God. Tides of opposition to the truth he presented arose, discouragement and despair had taken hold of him, and Timothy gave way to tears of discouragement.

In Jeremiah 9 the prophet who had been commissioned by God to give a message of judgment to the nation Israel gave way to tears. He cried, "Oh that my head were waters, and mine eyes a fountain of tears, that I might weep day and night for the slain of the daughter of my people!" (Jer 9:1). He had received a revelation from God of the horrendous coming judgment that would destroy Jerusalem and carry the people away into captivity. He came under such a burden because of the gravity of his message and the sufferings of his people, he could not refrain from tears.

The same thing is illustrated in the experience of the apostle Paul, in the book of the Acts. Speaking to the Ephesian elders from whom he thought he was taking his final departure, Paul said, "Therefore watch, and remember, that by the space of three years I ceased not to warn every one night and day with tears" (20:31). The apostle knew that false teachers would come to the assembly, and like ravenous wolves would destroy the flock. The tears of Jeremiah and Paul were tears of anxiety, of care and concern for those to whom they had been sent to minister the truth of God. So great was the burden of the message that the messengers experienced a broken heart because of the gravity of it.

In Mark 9, tears coursed down the face of a father. The record begins in verse 14. The father had brought his demon-possessed son to the disciples while our Lord was on the mount of transfiguration. The disciples were unable to deliver the boy from his demon possession, and, when the Lord Jesus returned to their company, the father approached Him and asked for help. Jesus said (vv. 23-24), "If thou canst believe, all things are possible to him that believeth. And straightway the father of the child cried out, and said with tears, Lord, I believe; help thou mine unbelief." Such was the burden of this father for his son that he pleaded earnestly with Christ, and the tears were a sign of his earnestness.

This is illustrated in Psalm 126:5-6: "They that sow in tears shall reap in joy. He that goeth forth and weepeth, bearing precious seed, shalt doubtless come again with rejoicing, bringing his sheaves with him." A careless, indifferent sharing of the Gospel with one who is lost will profit nothing. But when anxiety or earnestness are evidenced by tears, the psalmist promised the seed watered with those tears will produce fruit.

Tears may be an expression of desire. We read that after the children of Israel had been living by faith and had seen God supply their daily bread for two years, "The mixt multitude that was among them fell a lusting: and the children of Israel also wept again, and said, Who shall give us flesh to eat? We remember the fish, which we did eat in Egypt freely; the cucumbers, and the melons, and the leeks, and the onions, and the garlick: but now our soul is dried away: there is nothing at all, beside this manna, before our eyes" (Num 11:4-6). The children of Israel wept, but the tears expressed their desire for things that satisfied the flesh.

Tears may be a sign of devotion. As recorded in Luke 7:37-39, a woman came into the Pharisee's house where Jesus reclined, and brought an alabaster box of ointment. She stood at his feet weeping, and began to wash his feet with tears and wipe them with her hair. She kissed his feet and anointed them with ointment. When a Pharisee challenged Christ as to why He should receive the adoration of this sinful woman, He said that it was because she had been forgiven much. The forgiveness she had received produced a devotion that expressed itself not only in the gift of ointment, but also in the precious gift of tears. These were tears of devotion.

When our Lord looked out over Jerusalem, as recorded in Luke 19:41, He wept over it. These tears came because of the spiritual need of those He loved.

These Scriptures show that there are many different reasons why tears may come. In all but a few instances, these tears are not a sign of weakness. They are in most cases the evidence of a depth of feeling that brings delight to the heart of God. When one—for whatever cause—finds that tears are his portion, he has the promise of God: "Blessed are they that mourn; for they shall be comforted."

No tears were as hot as Peter's tears. In Luke 22, our Lord predicted that before the cock would crow twice Peter would deny him thrice. After his denial, "The Lord turned, and looked upon Peter. And Peter remembered the word of the Lord, how he had said unto him, Before the cock crow, thou shalt deny me thrice. And Peter went out, and wept bitterly" (vv. 61-62). No sorrow is as deep as that which comes to the child of God when he injures the love of the One who loved him unto death. There is no sorrow equal to the sorrow of injured love.

Yet even those who have injured the love of God by sin receive the promise, "Blessed are they that mourn: for they shall be comforted." In 1 Corinthians 15, we read what seems to be only a passing note; but how fraught with significance! In the record of the appearances of Christ on the day of His resurrection, Paul wrote that He appeared to Peter. The last time Peter had seen the Lord alive, he had felt His convicting glance. That glance had burned itself into Peter's heart, and Peter mourned. There was no comfort until the Lord appeared to him on the day of resurrection. Peter found comfort for one who mourned.

Think of the experience of David, in Psalm 32:3-5, "When I kept silence, my bones waxed old through my roaring all the day long. For day and night thy hand was heavy upon me: my moisture is turned into the drought of summer. I acknowledged my sin unto thee, and mine iniquity have I not hid. I said, I will confess my transgressions unto the LORD; and thou forgavest the iniquity of my sin."

David's words of confession are found in Psalm 51:

> Have mercy upon me, O God, according to thy lovingkindness: according unto the multitude of thy tender mercies

blot out my transgressions. Wash me thoroughly from mine iniquity, and cleanse me from my sin. For I acknowledge my transgressions: and my sin is ever before me. . . . Create in me a clean heart, O God; and renew a right spirit within me. Cast me not away from thy presence; and take not thy holy spirit from me. Restore unto me the joy of thy salvation; and uphold me with thy free spirit" (vv. 1-3, 10-12).

Then in Psalm 32, after David made his confession, he cried, "Blessed is he whose transgression is forgiven, whose sin is covered. Blessed is the man unto whom the LORD imputeth not iniquity, and in whose spirit there is no guile" (vv. 1-2). David had experienced tears of loneliness, rejection, frustration, and defeat. But nothing had so brought burden to his heart as the fact that he had sinned against God. Tears coursed down his cheeks, but he found, "Blessed are they that mourn; for they shall be comforted."

Think of the experience of Mary Magdalene recorded in John 20. She made her way after our Lord's crucifixion to the garden to find comfort in the place where His body had been laid. She "stood without at the sepulchre weeping" (v. 11). And Jesus said to her, "Woman, why weepest thou? whom seekest thou? She, supposing him to be the gardener, saith unto him, Sir, if thou have borne him hence, tell me where thou hast laid him, and I will take him away. Jesus saith unto her, Mary. She turned herself, and saith unto him . . . Master" (vv. 15-16). The tears were gone, and joy erased the sorrow. Mary found, "Blessed are they that mourn: for they shall be comforted." Mary found comfort in the presence of the Lord Jesus, and He erased what had brought tears to her eyes. She found Him "the God of all comfort."

Think of the experience of Daniel as recorded in chapter 9 of his prophecy. Daniel was a heartbroken prophet, weighed down with Israel's sin. In the first part of this chapter Daniel prayed a prayer of confession for the nation as though he had committed personally every sin which had brought about their expulsion from the land: "I set my face unto the Lord God, to seek by prayer and supplica-

tions, with fasting, and sackcloth, and ashes: And I prayed
unto the LORD my God, and made my confession and said,
O Lord, the great and dreadful God, keeping the covenant
and mercy to them that love him, and to them that keep his
commandments; we have sinned, and have committed
iniquity" (Dan 9:3-5). Here was a man who was
heartbroken because of the spiritual condition of his nation, which he assumed as his own, and poured out his
prayer to God:

> O Lord, to us belongeth confusion of face, to our kings, to
> our princes, and to our fathers, because we have sinned
> against thee. To the Lord our God belong mercies and
> forgivenesses, though we have rebelled against him;
> Neither have we obeyed the voice of the LORD our God, to
> walk in his laws, which he set before us by his servants the
> prophets. Yea, all Israel have transgressed thy law. . . . Now
> therefore, O our God, hear the prayer of thy servant, and his
> supplications, and cause thy face to shine upon thy sanc-
> tuary that is desolate, for the Lord's sake. O my God, incline
> thine ear, and hear; open thine eyes, and behold our desola-
> tions, and the city which is called by thy name: for we do
> not present our supplications before thee for our right-
> eousnesses, but for thy great mercies. O Lord, hear; O Lord,
> forgive; O Lord, hearken and do; defer not, for thy own
> sake, O my God: for thy city and thy people are called by
> thy name (vv. 8-11, 17-19).

The heartbroken, mourning prophet petitioned his God.
When He heard Daniel's prayer, He sent Gabriel, who
ministered in the presence of God to bring a message of
comfort to Daniel. Daniel mourned, and God comforted.

Our Lord did not promise, "Blessed are they that *moan*,
for they shall be comforted," but, "Blessed are they that
mourn." When we carry some burden that brings tears, our
natural response is to complain, to moan, to question
God's wisdom and benevolence, God's right to do this to
us. He did not say, "Those who moan will be comforted,"
but, "those who mourn." The biblical concept of mourning is recognizing a need, and then presenting that need to
the God of all comfort. When one, in desperation, oppres-

sion, loneliness, bereavement, discouragement, anxiety, earnestness, desire, devotion, presents his need to God, God commissions the angels of heaven to dry tears from his eyes.

God sent Isaiah to Israel to proclaim a message: "Comfort ye, comfort ye my people" (Is 40:1). Comfort for that beleaguered nation was found in a Person who would come to dry their tears. The Lord Jesus Christ came to the nation Israel in the fullness of God's time. He said, in Matthew 11:28-29, "Come unto me, all ye that labour and are heavy laden, and I will give you rest."

This same One has a ministry to the child of God today. In Revelation 7:16 John wrote, "They shall hunger no more, neither thirst any more; neither shall the sun light on them, nor any heat. For the Lamb which is in the midst of the throne shall feed them, and shall lead them unto living fountains of waters: and God shall wipe away all tears from their eyes." Again, in Revelation 21:4-5, "God shall wipe away all tears from their eyes; and there shall be no more death, neither sorrow, nor crying, neither shall there be any more pain; for the former things are passed away. And he that sat upon the throne said, Behold, I make all things new." The comforting picture John gave us of our eternal relationship to Jesus Christ is that He will so remove the cause that there will be no tears to course down cheeks again.

Our Lord, in Matthew 5:3, told us that our hope for the future can be our blessed experience today. When He walked among men, He was a man of sorrows and acquainted with grief. He was, Hebrews tells us, "tested in all points like as we are, yet without sin" (4:15). And because He was tested as we are tested, He is a merciful and faithful High Priest. He understands our tears. He invites us to Himself with the promise, "Blessed are they that mourn: for they shall be comforted."

3

Blessed Are the Meek

Matthew 5:5

The world does not see as God sees, nor does it think as God thinks. What is precious in the sight of God is often despicable to the world. Perhaps there is no place this is more clearly seen than in Matthew 5:5, "Blessed are the meek: for they shall inherit the earth."

What our Lord counts as the basis of blessing, the world utterly despises. The world equates meekness with an effeminate man, one who is mousy, a weakling, a pushover—yes, a coward. To say a man is meek is to treat him with contempt. Yet our Lord said, "Blessed are the meek for they shall inherit the earth." It is evident that our Lord has an entirely different view of meekness than what the world has.

For a biblical concept of meekness, look at the life of Moses. In Numbers 12:3, testimony is borne by the Spirit of God to the fact, "the man Moses was very meek, above all the men who were upon the face of the earth." When the Word portrays a meek man, it refers us to one to whom we would not attribute the character of meekness; yet God found meekness exemplified in Moses. When we think of him, we associate him with a fearless boldness. In Exodus 5, Moses, who had once fled from the presence of Pharaoh, returned to stand before the mightiest monarch of the world in his day. In Exodus 5:1, "Moses and Aaron went in and told Pharaoh, Thus saith the LORD God of Israel, Let my people go." Moses was not only unafraid to be in the presence of Pharaoh, but also he was not afraid to give

33

orders to one who ruled the nation. He did not go with a request; he went with a command. We see the holy boldness and the godly fearlessness of this man.

Throughout Exodus, judgment after judgment fell upon Pharaoh and upon his people and his land. Moses was not afraid to assume responsibility for those judgments. In Exodus 11:3 we read, "The LORD gave the people favour in the sight of the Egyptians. Moreover the man Moses was very great in the land of Egypt, in the sight of Pharaoh's servants, and in the sight of the people." Because of the boldness with which he called judgment from God down upon Pharaoh and the land, Moses gained a respect in the sight of the Egyptians exceeding the respect for even the authority of Pharaoh.

Exodus 32 reveals another facet of Moses' character. God had taken Moses up to the mountain and revealed the Law to Moses. He, in turn, was to transmit it to the children of Israel. But when he came down from the mount, he found them engaged in idol worship. "It came to pass, as soon as he came nigh unto the camp, that he saw the calf, and the dancing: and Moses' anger waxed hot, and he cast the tables out of his hands, and brake them beneath the mount. And he took the calf which they had made, and burnt it in the fire, and ground it to powder, and strawed it upon the water, and made the children of Israel drink of it" (Ex 32:19-20).

Here was an outburst of righteous indignation, that we can scarcely associate with a meek or timid man, against this godless worship which had sprung up in the camp. Moses was a man fearless in the presence of God and fearless before Pharaoh, a man who was given great authority and who exercised that authority even though it brought the wrath of Pharaoh down upon him. He was a man who could assume responsibility and faithfully execute it; a man whose soul could burn in anger when the name of his God was defiled and His Law disobeyed.

The world would never have called Moses a meek man, but God called him the meekest man on the face of the earth. Exodus 3 reveals what characterized Moses as a meek man, in the record of God's call to Moses out of the burning bush. There in the wilderness God revealed His glory to Moses; and God used a bush as a tabernacle in which to dwell temporarily and through which He might manifest His glory. Then God said to Moses, "Behold, the cry of the children of Israel is come up unto me: and I have also seen the oppression wherewith the Egyptians oppress them. Come now therefore, and I will send thee unto Pharaoh, that thou mayest bring forth my people the children of Israel out of Egypt" (vv. 9-10). This was the commission God gave to Moses.

Notice Moses' response—one facet of his character that caused God to call him a meek man. "Moses said unto God, Who am I, that I should go unto Pharaoh, and that I should bring forth the children of Israel out of Egypt?" (v.11). *Who am I?* He felt his inadequacy for this responsibility. He did not consider he had the capacity to do what God had commanded. To put it bluntly, he said, "Lord, I can't." Here is the first thing that reveals that in which God found such delight. Moses had no confidence in himself, no confidence in the flesh.

What Moses said of himself is what Paul later said of himself: "We are the circumcision, which worship God in the spirit, and rejoice in Christ Jesus, and have no confidence in the flesh. Though I might also have confidence in the flesh. If any other man thinketh that he hath whereof he might trust in the flesh, I more" (Phil 3:3-4). But Paul said that what he had such confidence in had been revealed to him as useless, and he had found that in himself dwelled no commendable thing in the sight of God. He concluded that in his flesh was no good thing (Ro 7:18). Paul and Moses had this in common: they could not and did not trust the flesh.

The second thing about Moses which caused God to call him the meekest man is in the fourth chapter of Exodus. After Moses had asked God to send some one along so that he would not go alone, "Moses took his wife and his sons, and set them upon an ass, and he returned to the land of Egypt; and Moses took the rod of God in his hand" (v. 20).

The rod of God was his strength in weakness, that upon which he leaned when he confessed he could not lean on his own strength. The one who said, "Lord, I can't," said, "Lord, You can," and he went, depending on God to do what He was sending him to do.

Further, "Moses and Aaron went and gathered together all the elders of the children of Israel: And Aaron spoke all the words which the LORD had spoken unto Moses, and did the signs in the sight of the people. And the people believed: and when they heard that the LORD had visited the children of Israel, and that he had looked upon their affliction, then they bowed their heads and worshipped" (4:29-31). Moses approached the elders of Israel to introduce himself as the deliverer as he leaned upon the rod of God.

We find a counterpart of this in Paul's experience. After he had said "I cannot trust the flesh" (Phil 3:3) he said, "I can do all things through Christ which strengtheneth me" (Phil 4:13). He wrote to the Galatians, "I am crucified with Christ: nevertheless I live; yet not I, but Christ liveth in me: and the life which I now live in the flesh I live by the faith of the Son of God, who loved me, and gave himself for me" (2:20).

Faith was to Paul what the rod of God was to Moses. As Moses approached Pharaoh with the rod in his hand, so Paul approached the ministry committed to him by faith, with no confidence in the flesh but total confidence in God. The conclusion is that Moses' meekness was not mildness of character, nor gentleness of disposition; but it was his distrust of himself, and his complete trust in God.

When our Lord addressed the multitude assembled before Him to learn from His lips the kind of righteousness necessary to enter into His Kingdom, and the kind of character that made one eligible for God's blessing, the Son of God said, in effect, "You must become like Moses, with no confidence in the flesh but total, complete confidence in God. Then God will fulfill His promises and bring you to your inheritance in the Kingdom that His Son shall establish on the earth."

Scripture gives us one other example of meekness. Paul said, "Now I Paul myself beseech you by the meekness and gentleness of Christ" (2 Co 10:1). As Moses was in the Old Testament the example of complete dependence upon God, so in the New Testament Jesus Christ became the example of meekness, of complete dependence upon God. Peter spoke of this when he painted a word picture of the Lord Jesus, charged with capital crimes, standing in judgment before a godless judge on trial for His life. He said, "Christ also suffered for us, leaving us an example, that ye should follow his steps: who did no sin, neither was guile found in his mouth: who, when he was reviled, reviled not again; when he suffered, he threatened not; but committed himself to him that judgeth righteously (1 Pe 2:21-23).

A cowardly Christ is inconceivable. He stood fearless before the multitides who sought to stone Him. His righteous indignation during the perversion of God's temple was such that He took a lash of cords and drove the moneychangers and those who bought and sold out of the temple, and possessed it in God's name. He was One who could fearlessly announce the judgment of God upon a guilty nation. Yet He was the meekest of all who walked the earth. His meekness was not mildness of disposition; His meekness was manifest through His total submission to the will of God.

Go with Him to Gethsemane as the shadow of the cross fell upon Him and He anticipated separation from God so that He might become a sacrifice for sinful men. He demonstrated His meekness as He sweat drops of blood, and said to the Father, "Not my will but thine be done" (Lk 22:42). Hebrews 10:7 records, "I come . . . to do thy will, O God." The gentleness and meekness of Christ was not timidity, nor cowardice, but a complete dependence on the Father.

It is this principle of submission that Christ emphasized when He said to those hanging upon His words and seeking entrance into His Kingdom, "Blessed are the meek: for they shall inherit the earth." "Blessed are those who submit for they shall inherit the earth." It is not by chance that those verses which described the meekness of Christ (1 Pe 2:21-23) were placed in the midst of Peter's extended treatment of the truth on submission. Men live in four distinct spheres of life. They live in the civil sphere; in the sphere of employment, the business sphere; in the sphere of the home; and in the sphere of the Church. Peter commanded submission to God-constituted authority in each one of these spheres. He said, "Submit yourselves to every ordinance of man for the Lord's sake: whether it be to the king, as supreme; or unto governors, as unto them that are sent by him for the punishment of evildoers, and for the praise of them that do well. For so is the will of God, that with well doing ye may put to silence the ignorance of foolish men" (1 Pe 2:13-15). Paul made it very clear in Romans 13 that human government was ordained by God and given the specific responsibility to preserve law and order and to maintain an atmosphere in which righteousness may flourish, so men may live without fear. To that end government was given the responsibility to punish lawbreakers. The Word of God commands the child of God to be in submission to government as it exercises its God-given responsibilities.

In the second place, Peter wrote, "Servants, be subject to your masters with all fear; not only to the good and gentle, but also to the froward [perverse]. For this is thankworthy" (1 Pe 2:18-19). Reaching into the realm of business or employment, Peter said the employee is to be subject to his employer, because the employer has the responsibility to curb lawlessness and maintain law and order in that realm.

In the third place, Peter wrote, "Likewise, ye wives, be in subjection to your own husbands" (1 Pe 3:1). God has constituted order in the home. The husband is to be the head, and the wife and children are to be in subjection to him. The husband has been given authority, as Christ's representative, to maintain law and order in the home. Believers are commanded to be in subjection to authority in the home.

In chapter 5, after describing the work and responsibilities of elders, Peter commanded, "Ye younger, submit yourselves unto the elder" (v. 5). Lawlessness can erupt in an assembly of believers as easily as in society, or in business, or in the home. It is the responsibility of the members to submit to the authority of the elders; such is divine appointment.

The sign of a meek man is that he recognizes divinely constituted authority and submits himself to every manifestation of it. He is subject to the authority of government; he is subject to the authority of the employer; he is subject to authority in the home; and he is subject to authority in the assembly of believers. Lawlessness or rebellion against any divinely constituted authority is lawlessness against God. One who is lawless is not meek, because meekness means submission to God and confidence in God.

The burden of Peter's epistle was that those who had witnessed the submission of Christ might manifest the same submission in every area of their lives so they might receive God's blessing. Lawlessness can never produce the fruits of righteousness in any area of life. Submission to God will bring God's blessing in abundance.

"Blessed are the meek: for they shall inherit the earth."

4

A Hunger for Righteousness

Matthew 5:6

Why is it that some Christians continue as spiritual babies, and others go on to spiritual maturity? We sometimes think it may be the difference in the individual personality, for some seem to be more religious than others and seem to have a desire for spiritual things. Sometimes we conclude it is a difference in a man's salvation or in his experience with Jesus Christ; for some had plunged deep into sin and have been brought out of its depths, and because of that great transformation, have gone on to spiritual maturity. Others think that because of early training—being brought up in a Christian home and learning of Christ from early years—men become more spiritual.

But when we turn to the Beatitude in Matthew 5:6 we find the secret of spiritual gianthood. Our Lord said, "Blessed are they which do hunger and thirst after righteousness: for they shall be filled." He stated that the secret of spiritual *growth* is a spiritual *appetite*. Those who eat little will grow little; those who eat much will grow much. Those with a voracious appetite for the Word of God and the Person of Jesus Christ, and who satisfy that appetite by feeding on the Word and by communing with the Lord, will grow to spiritual maturity, to gianthood.

A doctor can tell much about the progress of his patients by seeing how much they eat. Physical development is related to physical appetite. It is no less true in the spiritual realm. Spiritual growth, spiritual development, and spiritual health are inseparably united to spiritual appetite.

This principle is illustrated in the testimony of several spiritual giants, whose lives are recorded in the Word of God, who share with us the secrets of their hearts. Turn first to the experience of Moses. He had been called to Mt. Sinai, where God gave him the greatest revelation of Himself that any man had received since Adam's fall. God's holiness was revealed to Moses so that he might communicate it to the children of Israel. Moses returned from that time on the mount where he beheld the glory of God, and in obedience to the command of God he erected the tabernacle. When it was completed, Moses went into the tabernacle and into the presence of God. There he voiced a petition that reveals the deep longing of his heart. In Exodus 33:13, Moses prayed, "If I have found grace in thy sight, shew me now thy way, that I may know thee." Again (v. 18), "I beseech thee, shew me thy glory." All that God had revealed to Moses of Himself, instead of satiating him, had created in Moses a deep hunger to know more of the Person who had brought him to a relationship to Himself. He did not voice a prayer of thanksgiving, "I praise thee and thank thee for what thou hast revealed," but his prayer expressed the longing of his heart, "Shew me now thy way that I may know thee. . . . shew me thy glory."

In response to Moses' request, God set him in a cleft of the rock. Lest Moses should be consumed by the shining of God's glory, He interposed His hand between His glory and Moses. Under the protection of God's hand, Moses' longing was satisfied as God revealed His glory to him. That revelation came in response to the hunger, the longing of Moses' heart to know more. "Shew me now thy way, that I may know thee. . . . Shew me thy glory."

David walked in such close communion with God that he could pen the Psalms which have been a comfort to suffering saints through the ages, and have led them in their worship to the present day. He had entered deeply into the things of the heart of God, so that he could say, "The LORD is my shepherd; I shall not want" (Ps 23:1). He testified of God's nearness as he walked the paths of life. Yet David cried in Psalm 42:1-2 of the longing of his heart: "As the hart panteth after the water brooks, so panteth my soul after thee, O God. My soul thirsteth for God, for the living God." As a deer, pursued by natural enemies, driven to the point of exhaustion, longs with every fiber of his body for a refreshing drink from the spring, so David said, "My soul thirsteth for God." He testified again, in Psalm 63, to the same truth: "O God, thou art my God; early will I seek thee: my soul thirsteth for thee, my flesh longeth for thee in a dry and thirsty land, where no water is; to see thy power and thy glory" (vv. 1-2). The psalmist went deep into the heart of God, not because he was naturally religious, or because of some circumstance in his life. He entered deep into a knowledge of, and an experience with, God because He satisfied the hunger of his heart.

Paul recounted in Philippians 3, the great blessings he found in knowing Jesus, which superseded all one could know in Judaism. Even though Paul could look back on a ministry that had seen him bring the light of Christ to the Roman Empire, he cried out: "That I may know him, and the power of his resurrection, and the fellowship of his sufferings" (v. 10). *That I may know Him.* Paul was not satisfied with the result of his ministry, and he did not draw satisfaction from the fruit of his labors. His heart was not satisfied by activity. His heart was satisfied by communion with a Person. One of the tragedies of our day is that men try to lose themselves in activities, and to satisfy themselves by keeping busy. Paul said it was not the activity of the ministry that satisfied him, it was communion with a Person. It was the longing of his heart that he might go deeper into the things of God.

This was Peter's concern as he wrote to those to whom he was a spiritual shepherd: "As newborn babes, desire the sincere milk of the word, that ye may grow thereby" (1 Pe 2:2). In 2 Peter 3:18 he commanded, "Grow in grace, and in the knowledge of our Lord and Saviour Jesus Christ." Peter put a responsibility upon God's children to grow out of spiritual infancy and immaturity into maturity and adulthood. But Peter said that growth depends on an appetite. "Desire the sincere milk of the word, that ye may grow thereby." The Word of God was given to be to the soul what food is to the physical body. As loss of appetite indicates a serious physical problem, so loss of spiritual appetite indicates a serious spiritual problem.

The writer to the Hebrews wrote to a group of believers who had been saved a long time. They had endured suffering for Christ's sake and had been grounded in the Word of God so that they had been qualified to be teachers. But, according to Hebrews 5:11-14, they neglected the Word and the knowledge of the truth of Christ which they had possessed, and retrogressed into infancy, or, if you please, into spiritual senility. That danger confronts any child of God who neglects the Word of God and the Person of Christ. No situation concerns the pastor's heart as much as to trace the progress of spiritual retrogression in a man's life.

I can think of those who came to know Jesus Christ as a personal Saviour through the ministry of the Word, who evidenced the genuineness of their salvation by what seemed to be an insatiable hunger for the Word of God. A desire to feed on this living Bread brought them to all the services faithfully and expectantly. They asked the pastor for his recommendation of books they could study. Frequently the pastor's phone would ring early in the morning or late at night, and those who met something in the Word they did not understand would call so that he might share the truth with them. They gave every evidence of growing in the things of the Lord.

Then the phone calls would stop, and prayer meeting would fall by the way. Oh, they were there Sunday morning and evening, but the edge was gone from their appetites. Soon they receive all they feel they need in one service a week; then they are satisfied by an occasional visit. They have appetites that need to be satisfied, but they are not being satisfied by the Word. They open their ears and eyes to what is not food and let it pour into their lives. They give themselves to what can never satisfy. They bury themselves in business activity and leave the Word of God and Jesus Christ out. Spiritual retrogression sets in. Loss of spiritual appetite is a symptom of the most serious situation a child of God can face.

"Blessed are they which do hunger and thirst after righteousness: for they shall be filled." If you, before God, are convicted by the Spirit that the edge has gone from your appetite, or perchance the appetite is gone, on the authority of the Word we say to you, there can and will be no spiritual growth, development, no joy in your Christian experience, no power in your life until you return to the Word of God and the Person of Jesus Christ, and cultivate again that appetite which has been dulled or lost.

Hear again the heart cry of the giants: "Shew me now thy way, that I may know thee." "As the hart panteth after the water brooks, so panteth my soul after thee, O God." "That I may know him." "Blessed are they which do hunger and thirst after righteousness: for they shall be filled."

5

Blessed Are the Merciful

Matthew 5:7

Man rejoices in his own independence and likes to feel there is no situation in life he cannot handle. He takes great pride in sharing with others that he is a self-made man. Man wants a bootstrap religion, a religion in which he lifts himself up and makes himself acceptable to God. In spite of the fact the apostle teaches in Ephesians 2 that it is by grace and not by works that a man is acceptable to God, he holds onto this deception that he can work out his own salvation. He turns to a passage of Scripture such as Matthew 5:7, "Blessed are the merciful: for they shall obtain mercy," and convinces himself that the way to win friends and influence people is to be nice to them, and they will be nice in return.

"Blessed are the merciful: for they shall obtain mercy." From a casual reading of this verse it appears that the way to get along with people is to be nice to them; and the way to receive benefit from people is to bestow some benefit on them.

Once I received a large brochure from a radio preacher. He professed to have discovered the secret of the "tithe blessing." It was very simple: if I would send him a gift, he promised that a greater gift would come to me in return. He cited a number of examples of widows who had sent him all their material possessions and told how they had received greater possessions in return. He concluded by saying that the previous week one had sent him a thousand dollars, and now the one who had sent him the gift was driving a Cadillac. He based his reasoning on the proposition that if we give, we will always receive more back than we give. But this concept is based on a gross misconception of the human heart. The human heart is not so naturally kind and gracious and loving that it automatically responds to any kindness with kindness. The natural heart is selfish and tends to view one who is kind as being soft and as one who can be taken advantage of easily.

There is no better illustration of one who showed mercy than the Lord Jesus Himself. The record of His earthly sojourn is of One who was merciful. It is recorded in Luke 4:40, "When the sun was setting, all they that had any who were sick with divers diseases brought them unto him; and he laid his hands on every one of them, and healed them." Christ showed mercy to the sick and to those who had some infirmity. Once He stopped a funeral procession in which a mother accompanied her deceased son to the cemetery. He touched the casket and restored the young man to life and to his widowed mother. He showed mercy in sorrow and in death. John 8 records that when one taken in adultery was brought to Christ, and the leaders asked Him to sit as a judge and condemn her to be stoned, our Lord said, "He that is without sin among you, let him first cast a stone" (v. 7). The accusers slithered away, and the Lord said to her, "Neither do I condemn thee: go, and sin no more" (v. 11). This was mercy to the sinful.

On one occasion parents brought their little ones to the Lord so that He might lay His hands upon them and bless them. The disciples, irritated at the interruption, sought to send the parents home. He said, "Suffer little children, and forbid them not, to come unto me: for of such is the kingdom of heaven. And he laid his hands on them" (Mt 19:13-15). He showed mercy to the weak, the helpless, the infants.

On another occasion Jesus was eating in the house of Levi (Matthew), a tax collector. Many tax collectors and sinners also sat with Jesus and His disciples. "When the scribes and Pharisees saw him eat with publicans [tax collectors] and sinners, they said unto his disciples, How is it that he eateth and drinketh with publicans and sinners? When Jesus heard it, he saith unto them, They that are whole have no need of the physician, but they that are sick: I came not to call the righteous, but sinners to repentance" (Mk 2:16-17). He showed mercy to the outcasts, the rejects of society, the unacceptable ones.

From beginning to end, our Lord's life was a life of mercy. If mercy carried with it its own reward, there could have been no cross; but the merciful One obtained no mercy and was rejected and crucified.

Two merciless systems united to bring Jesus to the cross. First there was the imperial might of Rome, which at the time of our Lord enslaved sixty million people and subjected them to a system of law that was totalitarian. In spite of the fact that the Roman governor at Jesus' trial, six times over, declared Him to be innocent, yet he agreed to condemn Him to death. The merciless might of Rome did not respond to the mercy of Jesus Christ.

Rome was joined by the fanaticism of a merciless religious system that could tolerate no rebellion, no criticism, no competition. When our Lord said to the leaders, "Except your righteousness shall exceed the righteousness of the scribes and Pharisees, ye shall in no case enter into the kingdom of heaven" (Mt 5:20), they pursued Him and sought His death, and joined with merciless Rome and mercilessly demanded the death of the merciful One. Mercy does not always have its reward.

What then did our Lord mean when He said, "Blessed are the merciful: for they shall obtain mercy?" At the outset, we need to realize that mercy does not naturally belong to man. It is not a natural characteristic of the human heart. You can look in vain for a manifestation of mercy from natural men. Mercy belongs to God. Our Lord taught this in Luke 6:36: "Be ye therefore merciful, as your Father also is merciful." Mercy in man is an acquired characteristic which comes as a merciful Father produces His own life, His own nature, and His own character in His child. The psalmist said, "Unto thee, O Lord, belongeth mercy" (Ps 62:12). It is said twenty-six times in Psalm 136 that God's mercy endures forever. So impressed was the psalmist with the mercies that came from a merciful God that twenty-six times he extolled God, who is merciful and the fountain and source of all mercy. Mercy is God's loving grace in action. Mercy is God's response to the misery, to the need of one whom He loves. God loves not because the object of His affection is lovely and attractive to Him; God loves because it is His nature to do so.

In loving, God does not deal with us according to our sins nor reward us according to our iniquities (Ps 103:10). He deals with us not in terms of what we are, but graciously, in spite of what we are.

Love and grace combine in what Scripture calls "the mercy of God." The psalmist recognized that if God marked our sin, we could not stand in His sight. Because of our sinfulness we have no acceptance before Him. But God in grace sets aside what we deserve in order to give us what we never could deserve. The psalmist continued, "For as the heaven is high above the earth, so great is his mercy toward them that fear him" (v. 11). If you can measure the distance between the presence of God and sinful man, you can measure the mercy of God. It is limitless. But he pointed out that mercy does not originate in the human heart and proceed toward God; mercy originates with God and is showered upon men.

Shakespeare certainly grasped this truth when he said through Portia in *The Merchant of Venice*, "The quality of mercy is not strained." That is, it is not forced; it is not pried out of a person but "It droppeth as the gentle rain from heaven."

Mercy is unforced, or unmerited, as it comes from God upon man. That is what the psalmist had in mind when he said that mercy comes from God in heaven toward those that fear Him. "As far as the east is from the west, so far hath he removed our transgressions from us" (Ps 103:12). Here is God's great act of mercy to sinners. Recognizing that they were separated from Him, He separated their sins from them so that they need not be separated from Him. As long as the sinner bears his own sin, he is separated from God. When that sin is removed, he is no longer separated from God. As far as the infinite distance between east and west, thus far has God in mercy removed our sins from us.

"Like as a father pitieth his children, so the Lord pitieth them that fear Him" (v. 13). It is a father's heart to love and to care for his child. The heart of our Father is poured out in loving, gracious concern for those who are His children. Thus the psalmist has shown us that mercy originated with God; it is showered upon us from God; it comes to us not because of what we are but because of who God is. It is not a reward for what we are, but is an expression of God's loving, gracious concern for those who are the objects of His affection. We do not look for mercy from men in response to our attitude or actions toward them, for they do not have the capacity to be merciful. Mercy comes from God.

What did our Lord have in mind when He said, "Blessed are the merciful"? *Merciful* means "full of mercy." Just as a graceful person is one full of grace, the merciful person is the one who is full of the fountain of mercy, who is full of God. The merciful man is the man who is full of love, and who loves with the love of God. He is the man in whose life the cross has done a transforming work to conform him to Jesus Christ; that which is not a natural characteristic of his life becomes the character and pattern of his life.

What God expects of a righteous man is made so clear in an incident recorded in Luke 10, in which our Lord was tested by a lawyer. A lawyer in Israel was one skilled in the interpretation of the Mosaic Law, and also was an interpreter of the rabbinical traditions which had grown up around the Mosaic Law. This one so skilled came to Christ and said, in effect, "I know what Moses says about entrance into the Kingdom. I know the righteousnesses that the Pharisees say are necessary before one is acceptable before God. Now, what do You say?"

He put Christ to a test as to His interpretation of the standard of righteousness that God has for those who walk in fellowship with Himself. To put it simply, the question

was, "Just how good does a man have to be to please God?"
Our Lord did not answer the question directly but turned
to the lawyer and asked him what the Law said, and what
he believed to be God's standard of righteousness and
conduct. The lawyer knew the Mosaic Law, because he
could cite what God expects of a righteous man. He answered that God's requirement is, "Thou shalt love the
Lord thy God with all thy heart, and with all thy soul, and
with all thy strength, and with all thy mind" (v. 27). When
one is so controlled by love for God, there will be no sin
against God. The second requirement of one who is righteous is, "Thou shalt love thy neighbor, as thyself" (Lev 19:
18). One who acts in love toward his neighbor will be
guilty of no crime against his neighbor, so that love for
God and love for his neighbor will control a man's life and
he will live a righteous life which pleases God.

The lawyer stood convicted by his own summation of
the Law, for he had not pleased God. He had not loved God
and had not loved his neighbor. Conviction seeks a covering, an excuse, so he pleaded ignorance. He said in effect,
"The only reason I have not lived a righteous life is that I
do not know who my neighbor is. Now if I had that
clarified, I would be righteous."

The parable of the Good Samaritan was related by our
Lord to do two things: first, to show this lawyer who his
neighbor was; and second, to summarize what constitutes
righteousness in the sight of God. You know the story well.
A man going from Jerusalem to Jericho fell among thieves,
and the thieves beat him mercilessly, and robbed him of all
his possessions, left him alongside the road, abandoned
him to die, and went on their way with their spoils. In time
a priest came by. The priest saw the man, so he was not
ignorant. The priest recognized the man's need, so he
knew his responsibility, but he passed by and did not
recognize his obligation in the light of his knowledge.
Soon thereafter a Levite came by, and the Levite saw the
man; so he was not ignorant. He recognized the man's
need and knew his responsibility, but he was unwilling to
assume any obligation, and he passed by. They were fol-

lowed by a despised one, an outcast to the Jews, a Samaritan. The Samaritan saw the need, he recognized a responsibility in the light of his knowledge, and he poured oil into the wounds to soothe, and wine to cleanse, and he gave transportation to a haven of rest, and assumed obligations for the cost of caring for this man until he returned to health.

Then our Lord turned and said to the lawyer, "Which one of these three was a neighbor?"

Only one choice was open to the lawyer, and he had to confess, "The Samaritan who ministered to the need."

Our Lord first defined one's neighbor. My neighbor is not the one who adjoins me on the block. My neighbor is any man in need, whose need I know, which need I have an ability to meet. Righteousness demands a loving, gracious response to his need on my part or I am not fulfilling my obligation to either God or to man.

Our Lord concluded this word to the lawyer by saying, "Go and do thou likewise." What does God expect of a righteous man? Mercy: loving, gracious concern for the one whose need has been brought to my attention, which need I am capable of meeting. Mercy is the manifestation of righteousness.

When our Lord said, "Blessed are the mercy-full," He was saying that a man who has turned in faith to Jesus Christ and has received of His loving grace, received of His mercy, will be conformed to the mercy of Jesus Christ so that God's mercy can continually flow through his daily life. Righteousness before God brings the blessing of God upon a man's life. To show mercy because we have received mercy demonstrates the life of Christ, the work of the cross in a man's life, and permits God to open up the windows of heaven and pour out blessing upon us. A man whose life is lived by the love of God manifested at the cross will find his life flooded by the love of God. God, the source of mercy, has caused His mercies to flood my life through the cross. His righteousness will manifest itself through my life in loving, gracious concern. As His righteousness is perfected in me, His blessings may fall upon me. Mercy is the manifestation of the righteousness of Christ in the life of the child of God that opens a life to the blessings of God. "Blessed are the merciful: for they shall obtain mercy."

6

Blessed Are the Pure in Heart

Matthew 5:8

At the time of the coming of Jesus Christ into this world, Israel found herself crushed under the heel of an oppressor. She knew no political freedom. Rome had subjected that part of the world to its authority and ruled over Israel with an iron grip. The people longed for a political deliverer who would reinstitute the national life of Israel and bring them the blessing of freedom through his reign. Israel was oppressed economically, for the Roman Empire imposed taxes to support the empire upon people whom they subjugated, and the people were hard-pressed to meet their obligation to Rome. They looked for one to bring them liberty from such a burdensome economic oppression.

The children of Israel were also burdened religiously, for they were under the authority of the Pharisees who, misinterpreting the Law of Moses, had rigidly imposed upon the people a strict system of duties that they could not perform. The people looked for one who would deliver them from this religious oppression. They were burdened by a guilty conscience, for there was nothing in their political or religious system that could give the guilty conscience peace or make it whole again. The people cried for a redeemer, a savior.

One had been promised to Israel in the Old Testament, where God through the prophets had promised the coming of the Messiah who would deliver Israel politically and bring them under the beneficence of His rule. He had promised them a deliverer from economic oppression so that there would be bounty and plenty for all. He had promised deliverance from religious oppression, for Messiah would be a King-Priest and would institute a reign of righteousness which would cover the earth as the waters cover the sea. He had promised a Redeemer who would provide salvation from sin and bring men to peace with God. That hope had been treasured in the hearts of many in Israel through their long history as they waited for the coming of the Deliverer, the Messiah, the Son of God.

A revelation was made to Mary that she would conceive and bear a Son, who should be called Jesus, the Deliverer, for, "He shall be great, and shall be called the Son of the Highest: and the Lord God shall give unto him the throne of his father David" (Lk 1:32). Following the announcement to Mary, when Mary came to visit her cousin Elizabeth, Elizabeth was filled with the Holy Ghost and as a prophetess spoke, "Blessed art thou among women, and blessed is the fruit of thy womb" (Lk 1:42). God had said unto Abraham, "In thee shall all families of the earth be blessed" (Gen 12:3). When Elizabeth spoke as a prophetess, and said, "Blessed is the fruit of thy womb," she spoke of the Blesser whom God had promised to Abraham.

At the time of the birth of John the Baptist, his father, Zacharias, was fulfilling the role of a prophet, as recorded in Luke 1:67-69, 77: "His father Zacharias was filled with the Holy Ghost, and prophesied, saying, Blessed be the Lord God of Israel; for he hath visited and redeemed his people, and hath raised up an horn of salvation for us in the house of his servant David. . . . To give knowledge of salvation unto his people by the remission of their sins." This prophet-priest Zacharias had announced the coming of the hope of Israel.

The announcement concerning the coming of this One was made also to shepherds as they watched over their flocks by night, for the angels said, "For unto you is born this day in the city of David a Saviour, which is Christ the Lord" (Lk 2:11).

Simeon, ministering in the temple, was filled with the Holy Spirit when he saw the baby Jesus, and as a prophet he spoke and said, "Now lettest thou thy servant depart in peace, according to thy word: for mine eyes have seen thy salvation, which thou hast prepared before the face of all people" (Lk 2:29-31). The hope of Messiah's coming, grown so dim to so many, was stirred into flame.

As the years rolled on and the Messiah did not deliver from Rome and did not lift the burden of taxation, and did not deliver them from the oppressive system of the Pharisees nor from the guilt of their conscience, this hope again seemed to grow dim. Thirty years elapsed from the time the prophets at the time of His birth spoke of the coming of a Saviour until John the Baptist appeared in the wilderness again to rekindle hope in the hearts of the people as he cried, "Repent ye: for the kingdom of heaven is at hand" (Mt 3:2), and, "Behold the Lamb of God, which taketh away the sin of the world" (Jn 1:29).

When John introduced Him as a King, he was emphasizing that this One would deliver from the political and economic oppression of Rome, and would institute a kingdom of righteousness in which righteous men would find the peace and the provision of God. When he said, "Behold the Lamb of God, which taketh away the sin of the world," he was promising that the grip of Pharisaism would be broken and that God through the death of His own Son would provide a cleansing from sin and relief to the guilty conscience. John introduced the Deliverer who had been promised by God.

Multitudes pressed around the One whom John introduced to hear words about how a man could be made acceptable to God. The record of such a One is found in John 3, where Nicodemus, a ruler of the Jews, possibly conscious of his own unworthiness to stand in the presence of God, came to this One whom he recognized had come with God's message. He sought the answer to the question, How can a man be accepted by God? How righteous does a man have to be to stand in the presence of the Deliverer when the Deliverer sets up His Kingdom?

In response, the Lord stated God's standard and requirement very succinctly: "Except a man be born of water and of the Spirit, he cannot see the kingdom of God" (Jn 3:5). God is a holy God. He is a God of absolute righteousness. In Him is no sin, and the demand that God makes on those who would stand in His presence is no less than the unalterable holiness of God. This is a standard man cannot attain to, but nonetheless it is God's standard.

The multitudes who pressed around our Lord recognized their need for a political and a religious deliverer who would settle the sin question and give them a righteousness that would make them acceptable to a holy God. As our Lord went about all Galilee, as recorded in Matthew 4:23, teaching in their synagogues and preaching the Gospel of the Kingdom, healing all manner of diseases among the people, His fame went throughout the countryside. Those whose attention had been arrested came with hearts burdened with one important question: What kind of righteousness must we have before we can be accepted into the Kingdom of the Deliverer?

In the beatitude in Matthew 5:8, our Lord gave an unequivocal answer, "Blessed are the pure in heart: for they shall see God." If this positive statement is true, the converse is also true: "Woe to the impure in heart, for they shall never see God." This is the truth the Lord Jesus Christ gave them in answer to their question, "How good does a man have to be to be acceptable to God?"

Man measures himself by his fellow man. When he desires to test his character, his ethics, or his morals, he measures himself by fellow men. He can always find someone who is a little bit lower than he is, and measuring himself by another man, he congratulates himself that he has not sunk as low as some other man. What this means is that the ultimate standard of morality is the morality of the most debauched individual alive. The one you deem below you seeks somebody below him so he can congratulate himself. Thus, we work our way down the ladder so that the standard of morality becomes the standard of the most sinful person we can discover.

Not so with God. When God tests a man's character, his morals, his ethics, his standards, his acceptability to Himself, God measures the man by His own unchangeable, unalterable, absolute holiness. All that does not attain to the standard of the absolute holiness of God is unacceptable in His sight. Holiness is not something that we can compare—holy, holier, holiest. A surgeon who selects a scalpel in the operating room rejects a scalpel with a minute spot of defilement on it as readily as one that was severely defiled, because even the smallest spot means the scalpel is defiled and cannot be used in surgery. The degree of defilement is inconsequential. The fact of defilement is what matters to the surgeon. A thing is sterile or defiled, clean or unclean. A person is holy or unholy. God is not concerned with degrees. He is concerned only with the absolute.

This fact, presented to us throughout the Word of God, is found as early as Genesis 3. There we have the record of the first sin that intruded into this earthly creation. In the Garden of Eden, two creatures, who had been created with untried innocence, corrupted themselves by rebelling against the known command of God. Notice the immediate result of disobedience: "The eyes of them both were opened, and they knew that they were naked; and they sewed fig leaves together, and made themselves aprons" (v. 7). The nakedness was not before each other; the nakedness was before God. They recognized they were unacceptable in the sight of a holy God. They did not need an evangelist to convict them of sin; the Holy Spirit did that. The fact that they made clothes was a testimony to the fact that they were unholy and estranged from God. The clothing industry exists because it is written in the heart of man that he is unholy and unacceptable to God. The wave of nakedness and nudity that pervades our society is a vain attempt to deny that man is unacceptable to God, that man is a sinner. When one parades his nudity he says in effect, "I am completely acceptable to God." That is a lie of the devil.

The significant thing is, that which Adam and Eve fabricated did not satisfy themselves, let alone God. When they were walking in the Garden in the cool of the day and they heard God coming to enjoy fellowship with them, they went to hide. As they cowered in hiding, they were acknowledging they were unworthy to stand in the presence of a holy God because they were sinners. Adam and Eve fled from the face of God because of sin. This clearly illustrates the principle: "Blessed are the pure in heart: for they shall see God," and the converse, "Woe to the impure, for they shall not see God."

The psalmist taught us the same truth in Psalm 24. He pictured himself as a pilgrim going to Jerusalem to one of the annual feasts. His heart thrilled as he saw on the horizon the beauty of the city and the temple. As he approached the gates of the city and the sanctuary, his heart was smitten because of his own unworthiness to stand in the presence of God. He cried, "Who shall ascend into the hill of the LORD? or who shall stand in his holy place?" (v. 3). The answer came, "He that hath clean hands, and a pure heart; who hath not lifted up his soul unto vanity, nor sworn deceitfully. He shall receive the blessing from the LORD, and righteousness from the God of his salvation" (vv. 4-5). David said the only one who could approach the tabernacle as a worshiper was one who had clean hands and a pure heart. "Blessed are the pure in heart: for they shall see God." David had no innate purity to commend him to God.

Isaiah pictured this so graphically in his prophecy: "Behold, the LORD's hand is not shortened, that it cannot save; neither his ear heavy that it cannot hear; But your iniquities have separated between you and your God, and your sins have hid his face from you, that he will not hear" (Is 59:1-2). ("Blessed are the pure in heart: for they shall see God.") But the prophet said we are not pure; and God has had to hide His face. Throughout the chapter Isaiah recounts Israel's sins and summarizes, "Our transgressions are multiplied before thee, and our sins testify against us: for our transgressions are with us; and as for our iniquities, we know them" (59:12).

God "saw that there was no man, and wondered that there was no intercessor: therefore his arm brought salvation unto him; and his righteousness, it sustained him. For he put on righteousness as a breastplate, and an helmet of salvation upon his head; and he put on the garments of vengeance for clothing, and was clad with zeal as a cloke. . . . And the Redeemer shall come to Zion, and unto them that turn from transgression in Jacob, saith the LORD" (Is 59:16-17, 20). After the prophet had portrayed Israel's heinous sin, that caused God to turn His face and prevented them from coming into His presence, he promised the coming of a Redeemer, who would grant deliverance and forgiveness.

The prophet Ezekiel likewise portrays the promise of God:

> Then will I sprinkle clean water upon you, and ye shall be clean: from all your filthiness, and from all your idols, will I cleanse you. A new heart also will I give you, and a new spirit will I put within you: and I will take away the stony heart out of your flesh, and I will give you an heart of flesh. And I will put my spirit within you, and cause you to walk in my statutes, and ye shall keep my judgments, and do them. . . . I will also save you from all your uncleannesses (Eze 36:25-27, 29).

The prophet promised the coming of One who would do a divine work so that sinners who come to God might be cleansed and given pure hands and clean hearts, so they might come into the presence of God. "Blessed are the pure in heart: for they shall see God."

How like children we are! A letter from some friends told about their two small children. The mother commented that the children were at the stage where they could take a bath without ever getting wet. How childlike we are in thinking we can cleanse away the defilement of the heart without a bath, and render ourselves acceptable to God without coming in God's prescribed way, through the blood of Christ. This is the message that Christ was trying to get across to these multitudes, "You need a deliverer." A political deliverer? Yes. An economic deliverer?

Yes. A religious deliverer? Yes. But above all, you need a Redeemer who will grant cleansing from sin, for apart from holiness no man can see the Lord. "Blessed are the pure in heart: for they shall see God."

This beatitude has two important things to say. The first, that a sinner is totally unacceptable to God no matter how moral, and good, and kind he may be in the world's sight, because he cannot attain the perfection that belongs to God. Measured in the light of the holiness of God, he is unholy. Until one is as righteous in the sight of God as Jesus Christ is righteous, he may never stand in God's presence. He will only stand before God as his Judge and hear Him say, "Depart from me, ye cursed, into everlasting fire, prepared for the devil and his angels" (Mt 25:41).

Jesus came and offered Himself on the cross as a sacrifice for our sins. By His death He paid the price for the sins of the world, and God offers forgiveness for sins to anyone who will accept Jesus Christ as personal Saviour. Isaiah told us that our righteousness in the sight of God is as filthy rags (Is 64:6). That is the divine viewpoint. But Jesus Christ, by His death, takes away those filthy rags and clothes us with His own perfections. When God looks at the one who trusts Christ for salvation, God sees that one as He sees His own beloved Son.

So dear, so very dear to God,
Dearer I could not be,
For in the person of His Son
I am as dear as He.

So near, so very near to God,
Nearer I could not be,
For in the person of His Son
I am as near as He.

CATESBY PAGET

"Blessed are the pure in heart: for they shall see God."

But there is a second truth to be learned from this beatitude. Even though we have been redeemed by the blood of Christ and have been made a member of God's family, God cannot and will not have fellowship with us on the level of our sinfulness. Holiness is a prerequisite for fellowship. "If I regard iniquity in my heart," Psalm 66:18 says, "the Lord will not hear me." I cannot enjoy the light of His countenance and the joy of His companionship apart from clean hands and a pure heart. In 1 John 1:7 we are told, "The blood of Jesus Christ his Son, cleanseth [keeps on cleansing] us from all sin." And in 1 John 1:9 we are assured, "If we confess our sins, he is faithful and just to forgive us our sins, and to cleanse us from all unrighteousness." Holiness and righteousness are prerequisites to entrance into God's presence. That same righteousness is a prerequisite to fellowship with Him day by day. "Blessed are the pure in heart: for they shall see God."

7

Blessed Are the Peacemakers

Matthew 5:9

As we annually celebrate the birth of the One whose name is Prince of Peace, we are conscious that "there is no peace, saith my God, to the wicked" (Is 57:21). The world cries out for peace, but does not find it.

In Matthew 5:9 our Lord described the blessings He brought to men: "Blessed are the peacemakers: for they shall be called the children of God." It appears in this verse as though what the Scriptures said the Lord Jesus Christ would do—bring peace to men—He has committed to men, as though it were our responsibility to institute peace on earth. This beatitude has been so misused and so misunderstood.

Peace belongs to God. It does not belong to sinful man; for sinful men are in a state of alienation, both from God and from each other. One who is in a state of alienation either from God or from his fellow man cannot experience peace, because peace is the perfect harmony and tranquility that belong to God. God is a God of peace. Paul prays, "Now the God of peace be with you all" (Ro 15:33).

He is not only the God who is the source of peace but also He is a God at perfect peace with Himself, a God characterized by perfect harmony and tranquility. This peace belongs to God because God is One. In Galatians 3:20, the apostle states the truth, "God is one." Since God is One, there can be no disunity, no disharmony, no conflict within Himself. Yet man is separated from God by sin, and the very separation of the creature from the Creator, the

62

separation of man from God, makes it impossible for man to be at peace. He cannot be at peace with himself. He cannot be at peace with God. Peace is impossible until man is brought to reconciliation to God, until man is reunited with the God from whom he is estranged by his sin. The fact of this alienation is made so clear in Romans 5:10: "If when we were enemies, we were reconciled to God by the death of his Son, much more, being reconciled, we shall be saved by his life." This enmity came about because, "By one man sin entered into the world, and death by sin; and so death passed upon all men, for that all have sinned" (Ro 5:12). Adam sinned, and we have participated in his sin. Because we are sinners, we are alienated from God and there can be no peace until that enmity is removed, and that separation is resolved, and men are brought into harmony with God.

The first great peace which must be provided and established, then, is peace between the sinner and God. When Christ said, "Blessed are the peacemakers," He was not providing a special reward for patient diplomats. He was speaking of those who are themselves at peace with God, who bring a message of peace to men, that they might be brought into harmony with the God from whom they have been alienated. Blessed are those who announce to sinful men the fact that a Saviour has come. The angels who announced the birth of the Saviour were essentially peacemakers when they announced, "Unto you is born this day in the city of David a Saviour, which is Christ the Lord" (Lk 2:11).

To emphasize this truth, our Lord referred to a shepherd who had under his care a hundred sheep. As night fell, and he led his flock back to the fold, he discovered that one of his sheep had been lost out on the mountain. "If a man have a hundred sheep, and one of them be gone astray, doth he not leave the ninety and nine, and goeth into mountains, and seeketh that which has gone astray? And if so be that he find it, verily I say unto you, he rejoiceth more of that sheep than of the ninety and nine which went not astray" (Mt 18:12-13).

In the Lord's teaching, sheep are used frequently to represent the lost. Sheep are among the most unintelligent animals created. If lost, they will never find their own way back to the fold; if separated from pasture, they will never find pasture themselves; and if not led by a faithful shepherd to water, they will die of thirst. They need one to show them the way.

In a parallel passage our Lord tells that, when a lost one is found, there is joy in heaven because the lost one has been restored to his rightful place. Our Lord in the parable emphasized that man is alienated from God, that man will never find his way back to God without one to show the way. A man will never come to a knowledge of salvation without one to proclaim salvation to him. Man will never go from alienation from God to peace with God without a peacemaker. Recognizing the lostness of those in His day, religious as they were, the Lord said, "Blessed are the peacemakers: for they shall be called the children of God." Blessed are those who go as the Son of man went to seek and to save that which was lost, to lead them out of the wilderness into the safety of the fold.

Colossians 1:20 tells us that Jesus Christ came into this world to make peace by the blood of His cross. The only way a man can come to peace with God is through the blood of the cross. If men may come to God only through this way, men need to be informed of the way of peace.

It is significant to me that Paul, in each of his epistles, refers at the outset to the fact that God is the God of peace, that peace comes from God the Father and God the Son. There is no epistle written by Paul which does not mention that truth in its introductory sentence. Paul was impressed that God, who is at perfect peace with Himself, has provided for men who are alienated from Him to come to peace with Him. Paul recognized he had been appointed by the God of peace to be a peacemaker. As he traveled the length and breadth of the Roman Empire, he saw himself as God's peacemaker, who had come to tell men that Christ had established a way of peace by the blood of His cross, and that through the cross they might come to peace with God.

In 2 Corinthians 5:18-20, we discover that God has appointed us His peacemakers:

> All things are of God, who hath reconciled us to himself [brought us to peace with Himself] by Jesus Christ, and hath given to us the ministry of reconciliation [of being a peacemaker]; to wit, that God was in Christ, reconciling the world [bringing the world to peace] unto himself, not imputing their trespasses unto them; and hath committed unto us the word of reconciliation [the responsibility of being a peacemaker]. Now then we are ambassadors for Christ, as though God did beseech you by us: we pray you in Christ's stead, be ye reconciled to [come to peace with] God.

Three times in these verses Paul emphasized that we who have been brought to peace with God have been made peacemakers. We are to let men who are alienated from God know how they can come to peace with Him and experience His peace. To be a peacemaker, a man needs to know just one essential truth: Christ died for our sins and rose again the third day in order that we might come to peace with God. A peacemaker must know that truth, then impart it to men who are alienated from God.

Man is separated not only from God but from man, and believer may be separated from believer. Such is not the purpose of God. In Ephesians 4:3 Paul wrote that we are "to keep the unity of the spirit in the bond of peace." It is God's plan that those who have come to peace with Himself should live in peace, believer united with believer in an assembly of believers. Believers have an obligation to maintain the peace God has provided through the blood of the cross. Where there is strife and jealousy and discord, man is not experiencing the benefit of God's peace. A man, it is tragically true, may come to peace with God and not experience the outworking of that peace in his life so that he lives in the unity of the Spirit in the bond of peace.

After our Lord, in Matthew 18:12-14, spoke of the work of the peacemaker—bringing the lost to peace with

God—He spoke of the work of a peacemaker in maintaining unity in the fellowship of believers. Here our Lord laid down certain principles to be followed where there has been estrangement between believers. He said, "If thy brother shall trespass against thee, go and tell him his fault between thee and him alone" (Mt 18:15). Notice this is not the confession by a guilty party to one whom the guilty party has wronged. It is the step to be taken by one who has been wronged. The one who has been wronged is not to wait for contrition and confession on the part of the guilty and to remain in an estranged state until the guilty sees the error of his ways. Jesus said, if you have been sinned against, go and tell your brother his fault, between you and him alone. The one wronged is to go to the one who has done the wrong and show the offense privately so that there be no scandal in the assembly and so that other members of the assembly not be involved in this one man's offense. That is the first step to be taken. The one who sees or knows the offense of a brother and goes privately to that brother is a peacemaker, because he seeks to reestablish peace that has been disrupted by the action of the offender. Our Lord said, "If he shall hear thee, thou hast gained thy brother." Peace has been restored, and there is no further disruption in the life of the assembly.

If going privately to the brother does not bring the brother to peace, that is not the end of the matter. The one wronged is to take this second step (v. 16): "If he will not hear thee, then take with thee one or two more, that in the mouth of two or three witnesses every word may be established." Here the one who knows of the wrong or of that which would disrupt the unity of the Spirit in the bond of peace, is to take two or three witnesses so there may be a restoration. These three are peacemakers, and the blessing of God is promised upon them.

If he neglects to hear them, "tell it to the assembly," so the weight of the whole assembly may be brought to bear upon this one who has disrupted the peace of the body. If the man will not be restored to peace as the whole assembly becomes the peacemaker, this man is to be put out of the assembly. He is to be treated as a heathen man and a publican. Do you see how important it is in God's sight that the unity of the body be maintained?

Why is the maintenance of the peace of the assembly so important? Our Lord tells us, "If two of you shall agree on earth as touching any thing that they shall ask, it shall be done for them of my Father which is in heaven. For where two or three are gathered together in my name, there am I in the midst of them" (Mt 18:19-20). What our Lord indicated here is that answered prayer is conditioned upon unity between the one asking and the God from whom the petition is sought. If a man is not at peace with God, he cannot pray with any confidence that his prayer will be answered. If a man is not at unity with his fellow believer, he cannot be at unity with God. The disruption of the unity of believers brings about disruption of the unity between the believer and God.

This same truth is emphasized in 1 Peter 3, where Peter spoke of the relationship between husband and wife. Peter insisted that a right relationship must exist between husband and wife in the home, or prayers will be hindered. Where there is not perfect unity between husband and wife, there will be no answered prayer. This brings us to a vital, important principle: answered prayer depends not only on an individual's being at peace with God but also on his being at peace with his brethren in Christ. If our vertical relationship is not right, our horizontal relationship cannot be right; and if the horizontal is not right, the vertical cannot be.

The effectiveness of an individual's prayer and of a congregation's prayer depends upon the maintenance of peace. That is why our Lord said, "Blessed are the peacemakers: for they shall be called the children of God." Not one syllable in Scripture ever gives us hope that man will bring peace to this earth. Swords will not be turned to plowshares and spears to pruning hooks until the Prince of Peace, the Lord Jesus Christ, comes to earth and subjugates all to His authority. He has not transferred to us the responsibility to make peace among nations, but He has given us the responsibility to tell men who are aliens that they can come to peace with God through the blood of the cross; and He has given us the sobering responsibility to keep the unity of the body in the bond of peace.

You may be a peacemaker, and you may receive the blessing of God promised to peacemakers, as you tell men that Christ died, and as you seek to maintain the unity of the body in the bond of peace. "Blessed are the peacemakers: for they shall be called the children of God."

8

Persecuted for Righteousness' Sake

Matthew 5:10-12

A young man, to provide for the expenses of his sophomore year in college, planned to spend the summer in a logging camp. He had come from a Christian home and a very sheltered background. Knowing the profligate life of many of those who lived in logging camps, his parents sought to prepare this Christian young man for the opposition he would face and the persecution he could anticipate. They did not hear from their son often during the summer, so when he came home, they questioned him about the attitude of the men toward his Christian faith. He seemed surprised they should ask. He said, "Why they didn't give me a bit of trouble all summer. In fact, they never even found out that I was a Christian."

The desire for self-preservation is one of the major drives in our lives. Many of us are tempted in the face of opposition or persecution to veil that which would cause persecution. Our Lord anticipated this in the Beatitudes when He said, "Blessed are they which are persecuted for righteousness sake: for their's is the kingdom of heaven. Blessed are ye, when men shall revile you, and persecute you, and shall say all manner of evil against you falsely, for my sake. Rejoice, and be exceeding glad: for great is your reward in heaven: for so persecuted they the prophets which were before you" (Mt 5:10-12).

Our Lord, in the course of the Beatitudes, pronounced the blessing of God on the humble, the penitent, the submissive, those with a passion for holiness, the kind, the righteous, and those who reconcile the alienated. But our Lord reserved His double blessing for those who are persecuted. Direct your attention to that characteristic of righteousness which brings the double blessing of God, a willingness to take a stand for Jesus Christ in the face of opposition and persecution.

The Lord was speaking to a sinful nation, one which had received a revelation of the holiness of God in the Law delivered through Moses, but which had turned from the requirements of that revelation. Through adherence to Pharisaism, the righteousness demanded by the Law had been circumvented and a system devised to excuse ungodliness and lawlessness.

John the Baptist had preceded the ministry of the Lord Jesus Christ with his ministry of condemnation: "When he saw many of the Pharisees and Sadducees come to his baptism, he said unto them, O generation of vipers, who hath warned you to flee from the wrath to come?" (Mt 3:7). He had warned that the Lord Jesus Christ, whom he introduced, was a Judge, "Whose fan is in his hand, and he will throughly purge his floor, and gather his wheat into the garner; but he will burn up the chaff with unquenchable fire" (v. 12).

John had thundered his denunciation of sin. He had exposed the hypocrisy of the people and the godlessness of the nation. He had preached sin and judgment so that he might reveal the righteous One who could bring righteousness to those who turned to Him in faith. Those who accepted John's message had identified themselves with John and with others who had received John's message, had concurred in John's judgment on sin, and had confessed the need of righteousness from a Redeemer.

Those who received John's baptism were alienated from the nation. The people despised them because they had left the nation. In leaving the nation by being baptized with John's baptism, they were saying, in effect, that their need could not be met in current Judaism. They would find no righteousness that satisfied them or satisfied God in that elaborate system. They were saying they were leaving because they had found something superior. That which they left hated and ostracized them. Some had even suffered martyrdom at the hands of the religious system because they had left it for something of superior worth.

As our Lord spoke to those who were concerned about the matter of righteousness and described the characteristics of a righteous man, He concluded by saying that a righteous man must separate himself from unrighteousness, from a godless system, and must be willing to endure persecution from the godless ones, if need be.

In John 15, our Lord dealt with a similar situation as He spoke to the disciples on the eve of His crucifixion. These disciples had left their economic pursuits because of Him. They had moved away from the religious system in which they had been brought up because of the righteousness He offered. They had left family; they had left Pharisaism; they had separated themselves unto Him.

While He was with them they were sustained by Him. In persecution He was their defense. In need He was their source of supply. All that they needed they found in Him. But He was to be removed from them, and they would stand alone. Our Lord pictured them as a small, defenseless band, pursued by an overpowering adversary who would seek to destroy them. He sought to prepare them for the opposition they would face. So, in John 15:18, He spoke at some length on the hatred toward a believer in the world. There was no question in our Lord's mind of the fact of the world's hatred. He was assured of it, because the world is godless and sinful.

As a brilliant light is painful to the eye, so the light of God's holiness is painful to a sinner and he seeks to hide from it. The believer, placed in the world as a light, brings pain to the world. There can be no other response to him than that of rejection, persecution, bitterness, and hatred. So our Lord said, "If the world hate you [and the original text implies it most assuredly will], ye know that it hated me before it hated you" (Jn 15:18).

Then our Lord proceeded to give a number of reasons why the world would hate believers. The hatred is understandable and, in the light of what the world is, it is perfectly natural, logical, and to be expected. Love of the believer by the world is as unnatural as the love of the world by the believer is unnatural. The first reason Christ gave is, "If ye were of the world, the world would love its own: but because ye are not of the world, but I have chosen you out of the world, therefore the world hateth you" (Jn 15:19). When He said, "If ye were of the world," He was saying, "If you drew your standards of life from the world, patterned your conduct according to the standards of the world, took your inspiration from the world," the world would approve of you, because there would be unity between you and the world. If your life was centered in the center of the world's life they would approve. Because your life has a new standard, a new goal, a new center, the world does not understand. The world cannot understand a Christian; therefore, the world is baffled by what goes on in the heart and mind of a child of God. That which baffles, which they cannot understand or explain, they reject. The world remembers what you once were, how you used to do what they did, how you went where they went, how you conducted your life the same way they conducted their lives, how you had the same goals in life that they had. They were perfectly at home because they understood you; but now you have changed, and the whole direction of your life is altered. They cannot understand the change. It confuses them, it baffles them; and therefore they reject you.

In leaving the world system and accepting the standard of the Word of God, you are saying to the world, "I have found something in Christ superior to anything you have." It does not have to be verbalized, but the very fact that you cast off the things of the old life and accept things of the new life as your goals and standards, is mute testimony you have found something superior. The world interprets this as a superiority complex on your part and they hate it. They cannot accept that there is superior worth in knowing Jesus Christ, and that Christ is superior to the god of this world. But they misunderstand and misinterpret. The fact you leave them testifies to the superior worth of that which causes you to leave them. You have left the bosom of the world. They cannot understand why you have wrenched yourself away; therefore the world hates you.

The second reason Christ gave is in verse 20: "The servant is not greater than his lord. If they have persecuted me, they will also persecute you; if they have kept my saying, they will keep your's also." Jesus Christ physically left this world nearly 2,000 years ago, but the results of His coming into this world are as real to the world as though He had left yesterday. The hatred the world had for Him the day He was crucified is as strong today as it was then. The world has not relinquished, nor has it satisfied, its hatred of Christ in 2,000 years of bitterness. Since Jesus Christ is not personally present, the wrath of the world is vented on those who identify themselves with Him, and the world continues its hatred of Him by hating those who are His.

The hatred of the world is not so much hatred for the individual believer as it is a manifestation of the hatred of the world for Jesus Christ. Until the world is finally judged by the appearing of Jesus Christ, the great Judge, the world will continue to hate Him and those who identify with Him. That is why our Lord said, "All these things will they do unto you for my name's sake" (v. 21).

The third reason for the world's hatred is in the last part of verse 21, "They know not him that sent me." The world hates God and hates Jesus Christ because it does not really know Him. It knows Him as a Judge. It knows Him as One who convicts of sin, but it does not know Him. Because of its ignorance of Him, it hates Him.

The final reason is in verse 22, "If I had not come and spoken unto them, they had not had sin; but now they have no cloke [excuse, or covering] for their sin." This is the root of the whole matter. Jesus Christ came into the world as light, and light disrupts darkenss. Light dispels darkness when men who are in darkness come to the light.

Before the coming of Jesus Christ into this world, men had never seen holiness and righteousness demonstrated.

74

Men had looked at other men and had seen sin, but had not seen one who was absolutely holy and righteous. Men therefore excused themselves because they were like each other. But when Christ came into the world, He revealed what holiness is and what the holiness of God demands. Men could no longer excuse their sin because they had never seen holiness demonstrated. Instead of loving the One who revealed what righteousness is, and instead of turning to Him in faith to receive righteousness from Him, they crawled away into darkness, because they loved their darkness rather than light, and they hated the One who convicted them of their sin.

In John 16:7-8, Jesus said that the Comforter, i.e. the Holy Spirit, would come, and when He had come He would reprove (convict) the world of sin and of righteousness and of judgment. The Holy Spirit works through God's children, and the righteous, godly, holy, sanctified life of a child of God convicts the worldling of his unholiness, his unrighteousness, and his ungodliness. The transformed life of a child of God shows the worldling that righteousness has been provided by Christ and is available. The believer, then, becomes an instrument the Spirit of God uses to make men miserable about their sin and their godlessness. The world hates the instrument that reveals their godlessness to them.

When our Lord, in describing the characteristics of a righteous man, said, "Blessed are ye, when men shall revile you, and persecute you, and say all manner of evil against you falsely," and when He said, "Blessed are they that are persecuted for righteousness' sake," He was saying that when a man is transformed by faith in Jesus Christ, the world cannot but hate him. The world will never approve him, or commend him, or pattern their conduct according to him. The world will hate, revile, and persecute. To revile means to heap abuse upon. To persecute means to attack, perhaps even physically. The world will lie about the believer, "say all manner of evil against you falsely for my name's sake."

In John 16:2, our Lord told of some actions of these who

reject the truth of God against those who receive Him: "They will put you out of the synagogues; yea, the time cometh, that whosoever killeth you will think that he doeth God service." Christ's followers could expect physical persecution, even death. It was upon such that our Lord pronounced a double blessing.

Because we live in what has been called a Christian nation, after 2,000 years of preaching the Gospel of Jesus Christ, we have been deceived into thinking the attitude of the world toward a believer has changed. That is a lie of the devil. It has not been changed at all. The world can only hate a believer. We have somehow been duped into believing we can change the attitude of the world toward Christ and toward Christians. We have tried to live before the world so as to change their thinking. We have tried to make ourselves acceptable. We are trying to do the impossible. We might as well try to take off for the moon with only our own two feet to get us there.

If you want to escape persecution by the world, it is really quite simple. If you want to escape the animosity of the world, approve the world's standards, approve the world's righteousness, accept the world's ethics. Live as the worldling lives, and you can escape persecution. If you want to escape persecution, approve the world's religion. Don't tell a man he is lost outside of Christ. Let him believe there are many ways to God. Deny the biblical truth that Jesus Christ alone is the way, the truth, and the life. Commend him for his religiosity, for his churchgoing, and for his giving to charitable institutions. You can escape the persecution of the world if you do not separate yourself from the world, do not take a stand for Jesus Christ. Do not let anyone know you are a Christian. Go right along with them. In the office, hide the fact you belong to Jesus Christ, that you believe you are saved, and are assured they are lost. Laugh when they tell dirty jokes. Do not reprove sin; countenance it. Smile at their mockery and their blasphemy of Jesus Christ. Do no reprove them when they take His name in vain—accept it as commonplace, as though it were your manner of life too.

You can escape persecution. It is not too hard. But remember that our Lord said, "Whosoever shall be ashamed of me and of my words, of him shall the Son of man be ashamed, when he shall come in his own glory, and in his Father's, and of the holy angels" (Lk 9:26). He did not say He would disown those who ingratiate themselves to the world so as to escape persecution. He did say He would be ashamed of what His children had done.

The truth our Lord shared in this beatitude captured the heart of Peter, for he wrote that we have been begotten

> unto a lively hope by the resurrection of Jesus Christ from the dead, to an inheritance incorruptible, and undefiled, and that fadeth not away, reserved in heaven for you, who are kept by the power of God through faith unto salvation ready to be revealed in the last time. Wherein ye greatly rejoice, though now for a season, if need be, ye are in heaviness through manifold temptations: that the trial of your faith, being much more precious than of gold that perisheth, though it be tried with fire, might be found unto praise and honour and glory at the appearing of Jesus Christ (1 Pe 1:3-7).

Here were believers willing to identify themselves with the Saviour. They were unswerving in their devotion to Him and undeviating in their separation from the world; even though coals of fire were heaped upon them, they endured steadfast. They would not identify with the world to escape persecution by the world. Peter promised that at the appearing of Christ they shall be found unto praise and honor and glory. "Blessed are ye, when men shall. . . persecute you."

Joseph found this to be true. He was persecuted by his brethren for righteousness sake, and ended up in a dry well in the desert. God brought him out of that pit and made him prime minister of Egypt. Blessed are they that are persecuted.

Daniel found this to be true. For righteousness sake he was in the lion's den. God raised him up and made him prime minister in Babylon. "Blessed are ye, when men shall revile you, and persecute you."

Jeremiah found this true. He was cast into a slimy dungeon, and quicksand engulfed him. He was persecuted for righteousness' sake. But God lifted him up and made his name honorable as the prophet of God throughout the nation of Israel.

God calls men to separation to Himself; but in separating them to Himself, He separates them from the world, and they must expect the world's hatred. Doubly blessed are those who show this fruit of righteousness.

9

The Salt of the Earth

Matthew 5:13-16

Perhaps the words heard more around the dinner table than any others are *Please pass the salt*. Salt is a necessary ingredient in our foods, and our health depends upon a proper intake of salt. It is added to our food not only to make the food more palatable, but also to sustain the delicate balance in the body so necessary to health. Either too much or too little salt can cause an undesirable disturbance in our physical well-being.

Salt has been valued from time immemorial. Roman soldiers were paid in salt and, if one were derelict in his duties, he was said to be "not worth his salt." Salt was used throughout ancient societies as a sign of friendship, a concept that continues to the present day. In the Arab world, if one man partakes of the salt of another man, that is, eats a meal with him, he is under his protection and care. If a man's worst enemy came into his tent and ate of his salt, he would be obliged to protect and to provide for him as though he were his dearest friend.

Out of that idea grew the concept of a salt covenant, referred to in 2 Chronicles 13:5, where God speaks of a covenant of salt made with David. Before the days of a notary public who could authenticate the legality of a document, when two men entered into a business agreement, they would haggle over terms until they had settled on the agreement. Then they would eat salt or portions of food together; eating salt bound them together in what they called a salt covenant. This covenant established a contract that was not to be broken.

God prescribed salt as a necessary part of the sacrifices. "Every oblation of thy meat-offering shalt thou season with salt; neither shalt thou suffer the salt of the covenant of thy God to be lacking from thy meat-offering: with all thine offerings thou shalt offer salt" (Lev 2:13). God said that if they left salt out of their offering to God, it was an unacceptable offering. The offering demanded the whole, and the offering was incomplete without salt.

Job refers to salt as a necessary ingredient of food as he asked the question, "Can that which is unsavory be eaten without salt? or is there any taste in the white of an egg?" (Job 6:6). As early as Job's time, men recognized the importance of salt, and attached special significance to it.

When the Lord said to the disciples, "Ye are the salt of the earth" (Mt 5:13), He spoke of the commonplace, yet that which in their experience had great significance. If salt had lost its saltiness it was only sand, and sand was valueless. The Lord spoke here of a quality of life that was to be evident in those who knew Him, had been taught His truth, and had put faith in Him. They were to become the salt of the earth.

In our society, in addition to using salt for palatability, we think of salt as a preservative. Before the days of refrigeration, meat to be preserved was submerged in brine, or rubbed with salt and cured. Our forefathers trecking across the prairie depended on salted meat for their sustenance. Because of this common concept we view this passage as the Lord teaching that believers are preservatives. Some think that, because of the presence of believers in this world, this world is spared from judgment, and that this world is a good place because believers are in the midst of it. This thinking is based on an erroneous concept of what the world is in the sight of God. The world is utterly corrupt, and the world system is under divine judgment, and God is not in the business of preserving this godless world. It is destined for condemnation. When Christ said, "Ye are the salt of the earth," He was not saying He had put them in the midst of corruption to purify what had been contaminated.

The primary function of salt is to create a thirst. Without salt in food, there would be an improper intake of liquid; and where there is an improper intake of liquid, there would be dehydration leading to sickness or death. This would be particularly true in the desert countries around the land where the Lord was speaking. If a traveler did not partake of the proper amount of water, he would suffer dehydration and death as he journeyed. Therefore, an essential part of every traveler's baggage was a sack of salt to prevent dehydration and its consequences.

We know something of this even in our day. Those who labor manually in the summer use salt tablets. Those tablets create a thirst so as to prevent dangerous dehydration. But if a tablet of white sand were substituted for the salt, dehydration would be the inevitable result. When our Lord said "Ye are the salt of the earth," He was saying He had put them into this world so that they might create a thirst for Himself in the life and experience of those who are dying because they do not know the fountain of living water. A believer's function is to create a thirst for Jesus Christ.

The Lord had said earlier, "Blessed are they which do hunger and thirst after righteousness: for they shall be filled." Without an appetite, there will be no eating, and without eating there will be no sustaining. Remove the appetite, and death is the inevitable result. The Lord told these disciples that He had put them there so their lives might be as salt to those whose lives they touch; so what was heard from their lips and seen in their lives would create a hunger and thirst for Christ that would drive men to Him to receive the water of life. No thirst, no drinking; and no drinking, no life.

This is made so clear in an incident recounted in Mark 10. While the Lord was traveling to Jericho He met blind Bartimaeus, who cried, "Jesus, thou son of David, have mercy on me" (v. 47). Those present sought to quiet this one who begged Christ to show mercy, but Christ called him to Himself. They brought Bartimaeus to Christ. "Jesus answered and said unto him, What wilt thou that I should do unto thee?" (v. 51). Until blind Bartimaeus recognized a need, there was no way that Christ could meet that need. So He brought from Bartimaeus a confession of his need. "Lord, that I might receive my sight." In response to his desire to see, Christ healed Bartimaeus.

The principle is so clear. Christ can and will do for a man what a man recognizes as his need. Until a man recognizes he is lost, he will have no desire to be saved; until a man recognizes he is ungodly, he will have no desire for godliness; until a man recognizes he is separated from God, he will have no desire for a bridge to span that separation. Without an appetite there is no petition. Without a petition there is no action. God has placed believers in the presence of unsaved men so that by our words and lives they might have a hunger created in them for that which has satisfied us.

To supplement this teaching, the Lord used a second figure, "Ye are the light of the world" (v. 14). The nature of light is to shine. There is no such thing as light that does not communicate itself. There is no such thing as self-contained light. Light may originate in a distant star and travel a span of light-years, but it does not get tired of shining and cease to shine. Its nature is to shine. Christ says He has made us lights in the world, and we are not self-contained. It is the nature of the child of God who has been made light to communicate the light given to him. One who travels in the Holy Land is impressed with the fact that multitudes of villages were built on the tops of the hills, where they could be cooled by breezes. There they could best defend themselves from invaders. When night came, the light in the houses on the hill could not be hidden. From a great distance, one knew the location of the next village because of the light from that hilltop.

Although we devise methods of blackout in wartime, the Lord said that a city set on top of a hill simply cannot be hidden. It is inconceivable that a man would light an oil lamp only to put it under a measure or hide it under a bed so that the light does not shine. The light is lit so that it might shine.

We have become vehicles through which light shines so that men who have had a hunger and thirst for Christ created in them might know the way. It is one thing to tell a man he is lost; it is another to tell a man the way out of his lostness. It is one thing to tell a man he is guilty, and another to show that man how his guilt can be removed. It is one thing to tell a man he is godless, another to show him the way of godliness. So these two figures supplement each other. The believer as salt creates a desire in the man who is in darkness for something other than what he has, but the believer's light shows him how his hunger and thirst can be satisfied. A believer is not either salt or light, he is salt *and* light. He creates the appetite and then shows the way that appetite can be met.

Paul emphasized this same truth in Philippians 2:14-16: "Do all things without murmurings and disputings: that ye may be blameless and harmless, the sons of God, without rebuke, in the midst of a crooked and perverse [distorted] nation, among whom ye shine as lights in the world; holding forth the word of life, that I may rejoice in the day of Christ that I have not run in vain, neither labored in vain." Paul made it very clear that the believer has been given light and is to let the light shine by holding forth the Word of life. To communicate the Word of God is to let light shine. To live the Scriptures before men is to let light shine. If a believer has been made light, it is because of the ministry of the Word in his life. The shining of the Word of God is the light in the believer's life. Paul pointed out that our relationship to the Word of God is such that we must discharge our responsibility as lights in the world.

This figure portrays the world as being in darkness and without light, and it shows the believer as light in the midst of darkness. Since it is the nature of light to communicate itself, God says He purposes that the Word of God that has made us light should be communicated through us, so that men in whose life a hunger and thirst for righteousness has been created might come to light.

John's Gospel deals with this same subject. We are introduced to John the Baptist, who appeared in the midst of moral and religious darkness. His coming was a fulfillment of the promise of the Word of God, "There was a man sent from God, whose name was John [the Baptist]. The same came for a witness, to bear witness of the Light, that all men through him might believe. He was not that Light, but was sent to bear witness of that Light" (Jn 1:6-8).

John came as a light, not to attract to himself but to reflect the light given to him so that men might be drawn through him to the source of light. The apostle John saw the Baptist as a light who reflected the Light. His ministry was not to attract men to himself but to the Light. That is why, when men came to John and asked if he were Messiah, he said he was not. He was a light to bring men to Christ.

John, by his preaching, was also salt. He created a hunger and thirst, but the very creation of hunger and thirst does not guarantee that man will have his thirst satisfied. He must be pointed to the Way, to the fountain of life. So John was light who showed those who had become hungry and thirsty for righteousness where the springs of living water flowed.

When the Lord spoke to this multitude, He said to them, in effect, "They who receive My word are to do what John the Baptist did. By your words and by your life you are to create a thirst for Me; and lest men stumble in darkness in searching for Me, you show them the way. Then bring them to Me, the fountain of living waters, so their thirst might be slaked, and let the light shine so men might themselves find the source of Light.

One semester we admitted a blind student to the seminary. I noticed that as he went from class to class, or dorm room to dining room, someone held his arm and guided him to his destination. The one who took his arm was his light, and he walked in the light of another.

The world in which we live is blind. If all men were blind, the blind would have no desire for anything other than their blindness. But because you see, you create a desire in a blind man for that which he does not have but which you have; then you become light to the one who is blind to lead him to One who is the Light of the world.

You are salt to make a man thirst for Jesus Christ. You are light to bring a man to Christ. If your pattern of life is so like the pattern of life of the unsaved man that he cannot see any difference between himself and you, you will never create a thirst in him for what you have. Salt does not serve its function by being just like the food on which it is placed. Salt has to be different to serve its purpose. Until there is a transformation in your daily conduct, you will never be salt. Apart from the Word of God you can never be light. God calls us from a world from which we were saved to a new kind of life so we might be salt. He delivered the Word to us so that we might be light to men who are lost.

10

How Good Does a Man Have to Be to Go to Heaven?

Matthew 5:17-20

How good does a man have to be to go to heaven? No man is so depraved that he thinks bad people go to heaven. He instinctively recognizes that heaven is reserved for good people. So the question is not, Will bad people go to heaven? The question is, Just how good do good people have to be to go to heaven?

That is the question our Lord faced when He spoke to the multitude assembled to hear His word:

> Think not that I am come to destroy the law, or the prophets: I am not come to destroy, but to fulfil. For verily I say unto you, Till heaven and earth pass, one jot or one tittle shall in no wise pass from the law, till all be fulfilled. Whosoever therefore shall break one of these least commandments, and shall teach men so, he shall be called the least in kingdom of heaven: but whosoever shall do and teach them, the same shall be called great in the kingdom of heaven. For I say unto you, That except your righteousness shall exceed the righteousness of the scribes and Pharisees, ye shall in no case enter into the kingdom of heaven (Mt 5:17-20).

Jesus Christ was introduced to the nation of Israel as their Messiah, their Saviour, and their King. John the Baptist introduced Him to the nation as the Lamb of God that taketh away the sin of the world, the Saviour. He also announced that the Kingdom of heaven was at hand. Jesus was the Sovereign. When one runs for office, to ingratiate himself to those over whom he hopes to gain authority, he makes all manner of promises. In an election year, we are deluged with promises. Men are wont to determine who shall receive their vote by who makes the most grandiose promises. But when Jesus came to offer Himself as a King, He did not seek to be received as King by making grandiose promises, or by promising them an easy way. Instead, He reversed the universal custom of those seeking office. Instead of making things easy, He made things hard, for the Lord said, "Think not that I am come to destroy the law and the prophets, I am not come to destroy but to fulfill." Christ did not require less than the Law but demanded all the Law required.

James, who understood the Law so clearly, gave a summary statement of what the Law demanded, "Whosoever shall keep the whole law, and yet offend in one point, he is guilty of all" (Ja 2:10). The Law demanded absolute, perfect obedience. If a man kept the entire Law, but violated one minute point, in the eyes of the Law he was a lawbreaker, and the sentence of guilt had to be passed upon him. The Law demanded absolute perfection.

When the Jews gave ear to the Words of the Lord Jesus, they came to Him as those who understood the demands of the Law. They stood condemned and convicted in the light of the requirement of the Law, and they sought a way of escape. They hoped He would set aside the Law, and the holiness and perfection the Law demanded, and that He would offer a substitute way, an easier way into the presence of God.

Had He set aside that which they were unable to perform, and offered them an easier way into the presence of God, they would have accepted Him gladly. But our Lord said, "I have not come to set aside in any way that which the Law demands. I have come to demand that the Law be fulfilled in every respect." For our Lord said, "Till heaven and earth pass, one jot or one tittle shall in no wise pass from the law, until all be fulfilled."

The Lord was using a figure very familiar to those accustomed to writing in Hebrew or Aramaic. The smallest letter in the Hebrew alphabet, made with a single stroke of the pen, was the *yod*, or the jot. Not one letter of one word shall fail in its fulfillment. To make it more graphic, our Lord said, "Not one tittle shall pass from the Law." Two characters in the Hebrew alphabet are identical in form, except one of them has a minute projection used in forming the letter. Instead of the letter beginning at the perpendicular line, it begins slightly to the left so that it crosses the perpendicular line in being formed. That minute projection is called a tittle. So our Lord said that not only will not one letter of the Law be relaxed, but also not even one almost indistinguishable portion of one letter will be relaxed. Those are His requirements.

Go for a moment back into the Old Testament and see what the Law was in its essential character. What was the Law designed to do? "Joshua said unto the people, Ye cannot serve the LORD: for he is an holy God; he is a jealous God, he will not forgive your transgressions nor your sins" (Jos 24:19). Hannah's prayer was, "There is none holy as the LORD" (1 Sa 2:2). Leviticus 21:8 reads, "Thou shalt sanctify him therefore; for he offereth the bread of thy God; for he [the priest] shall be holy unto thee; for I the LORD, which sanctify you, am holy." That which the angels cried in Isaiah 6:3, "Holy, holy, holy is the LORD of Hosts," is revealed to men on the earth through the Law.

All angelic creation beholds the holiness of God; but fallen, sinful men, because of their blindness and separation cannot behold the holiness of God without being consumed by it. God therefore revealed His holiness by reflecting it in a mirror. The Law was a mirror to reflect the holiness of God to men, but at the same time to protect them from being consumed by the brightness of God's glory. Mankind could know that God is a holy God through the revelation in the Law. Sin is sin, not simply because it injures society, or an individual in society, or the one committing the sin. Sin is sin because it is unlike the holiness of God. Such is Paul's definition in Romans 3:23, "All have sinned, and come short of the glory of God," that is, the glory of His holiness. Anything unlike the holiness of God is sin. Since men see only the reflected glory of God, and have only a reflected revelation of the holiness of God, it was necessary that God spell out for them what their conduct in life should be. So the Law not only revealed the holiness of God but also it revealed the demands a holy God makes of those who would walk in fellowship with Him.

Leviticus 11:44 reads, "I am the LORD your God: ye shall therefore sanctify yourselves, and ye shall be holy; for I am holy." Men were required to be holy in their manner of life because God is holy. Peter quoted this in 1 Peter 1:15 when he applied this principle to the conduct of believers. God is a holy God. God demands holiness of those who would walk to please Him. The requirements for holiness are spelled out for us in the commandments and prohibitions of the Word of God.

We find the same truth in Leviticus 19:2, "Speak unto all the congregation of the children of Israel, and say unto them, Ye shall be holy: for I the LORD your God am holy." Or, "Sanctify yourselves therefore, and be ye holy: for I am the LORD your God" (20:7); or "Ye shall be holy unto me: for I the LORD am holy, and have severed you from other people, that ye should be mine" (20:26). This revelation was given to Israel so they would know God is holy and so they would know the demands a holy God made upon them. But no man could by himself attain the holiness of God, nor could he walk in the precepts of God so he became acceptable to God. The Law passed a sentence of guilt upon all men who looked into it, "For whosoever shall keep the whole Law but offend in one point, he is guilty of all." The nation bore the weight of guilt.

Pharisaism was a clever system devised to circumvent the requirements of the holiness of God and the demands of the Law. The Pharisees had the Law in their hand. They knew the revelation of the holiness of God revealed there. They knew the requirements of God as to the conduct of righteous men, but they realized they could not attain that standard. Therefore, they devised a system which essentially circumvented the requirements of the Law to make it possible for men to attain a substitute set of standards. The Pharisees said that if one lived up to their interpretation of the Law, they would be acceptable to God.

The Pharisees had codified the Scriptures into 365 negative commandments and 250 positive commandments, and taught that if men kept all these, they would be acceptable in the sight of God. But every one of the commandments they had set before men had to do with external conduct. They were concerned only with external acts. They had interpreted the Law of God to apply only to outward acts, never to the thoughts that produced the act. They said it is wrong to murder a man, but said nothing about the hate that produces murder. They said it is wrong for a man to commit adultery, but nothing about the lust that produces adultery. They said it is wrong to steal, but said nothing about the covetousness which leads a man to steal. As long as a man was not caught in some *act*, he was righteous in the sight of the Pharisees.

Such a system falls infinitely short of the demands of the holiness of God. The nation groaned under Pharisaic tradition and found itself incapable of measuring up even to Pharisaic interpretation of the Law. The people looked for someone to deliver them from the burden of Pharisaism. As they hung upon the words of Christ, they hoped He would sweep away their responsibility to measure up to the traditions of the Pharisees and to the inviolable demands of the Law so they could be accepted by God as they were.

This conflict is seen so clearly in Mark 7, where the Lord dealt with this problem of Pharisaism. He warned the disciples against the doctrine of the Pharisees: "In vain do they worship me, teaching for doctrines the commandments of men" (v. 7). Pharisaism originated with men, not with God. For "Laying aside the commandment of God [the Law, which was inviolable and inflexible], ye hold the tradition of men, as the washing of pots and cups [concerned only with externalities and not with the heart]. . . .

Full well ye reject the commandment of God, that ye may keep your own tradition" (vv. 8-9).

He showed that Pharisaism is contrary to the Word of God. Then He gave a specific illustration. "Moses said, honor thy father and mother; and, Whoso curseth father or mother, let him die the death; but ye say, If a man shall say to his father or mother, it is Corban, that is to say, a gift, by whatever thou mightest be profited by me; he shall be free. And ye suffer him no more to do ought for his father or his mother; Making the word of God of none effect through your tradition, which ye have delivered: and many such like things do ye" (vv. 10-13). According to the Law of Moses, when a father or mother was aged and infirm and unable to support himself, it was the responsibility of the children to support the parent. That was a God-given responsibility. It would cost money to support the parents. The Pharisees, who loved money, did not want to contribute to the support of the parents according to their need, even though the Law said they were obligated to; so Pharisaism devised a way to circumvent the Law.

The Law said that something devoted to God cannot be returned to secular usage. A pot or a vessel, consecrated to the Lord's service in the tabernacle, could not, when it had outlived its usefulness, be used in the home. It had to be destroyed because it was God's. An animal offered to God as a sacrifice had to be bound with cords to the horns of the altar and could not be restored to the flock to be used by the offerer again. It was God's. So the Pharisees devised a formula whereby they pronounced the word Corban, which means "a gift" or "consecrated to God." So they would say everything they had was God's, and they had no right to use it themselves.

When a knock came at the door and the son saw it was his indigent father coming for help, he would realize he was going to have to part with some things he loved so dearly. As he went to the door, he would say, "Corban," all is devoted to God. He would throw open the door, see his father, embrace him, profess his love, and bring him into the house. He would inquire, "Father, what can I do for you?"

The father would say, "Son, your mother and I are destitute. We have nothing with which to buy food, and we are asking you to fulfill your filial responsibility to us."

With crocodile tears the son would say "Oh, I wish I had known, I have just devoted everything I have to God, and you know the Law will not let me take back from God what I have devoted to Him." The father would depart with his needs unmet.

The Pharisees approved this. A father could leave the son's house to perish in hunger, and the son could retain what was his with Pharisaic blessing. They counted that righteousness. Our Lord showed that by their practice they had circumvented the Law of God and yet called it righteousness. Our Lord went on in Mark 7 to show it is not what enters a man from the outside which defiles but what comes from within the heart of man that defiles, "For from within, out of the heart of man, proceed evil thoughts, adulteries, fornications, murders, thefts, covetousness, wickedness, deceit, lasciviousness, an evil eye, blasphemy, pride, foolishness. All these evil things come from within, and defile the man" (vv. 21-23). The source of defilement in the sight of God is not what is outside but what is inside.

Gathered here to hear the word of the Lord, were a people, who acknowledged their guilt, their uncleanness in the sight of God; they confessed their inability to measure up to the standards of God's holiness, but were looking for an easy way out, in the hope Christ would offer them an easy way. He told them that Pharisaic righteousness would never bring them into the presence of God. You would have to say the Pharisees were good men. As the world counts goodness, they behaved themselves, they were moral, they were upright, they were religious. But Christ said, "Except your righteousness shall exceed the righteousness of the scribes and Pharisees, you shall in no case enter into the kingdom of heaven."

How good must one be to be accepted? The Lord said, "One jot or one tittle shall not pass until it all be satisfied." Our Lord was saying that to be accepted into heaven one must be as good as the holiness of God revealed in the Law. That is how good a man must be to go to heaven—as good as God. We stand guilty and condemned before God, for unless a man keeps the whole Law he is guilty. But in the grace of God through the death of Jesus Christ, a righteousness has been provided for guilty sinners. Blood has been shed to wash away the stain of every sin. Righteousness imparted makes a man as righteous as Jesus Christ is righteous, so that a holy God can look at the one who stands in Jesus Christ and say, "That one is acceptable in My sight." *Accepted in the beloved.* There is no greater word in all the gospel than that. We have been accepted by a holy, righteous God to stand in His presence.

The Pharisees, who recognized the need for righteousness, sought to provide righteousness by their works. They failed. Christ rejected them and their righteousness. Their only alternative was to receive righteousness from Him. Men today are faced with the same alternatives. They either must provide righteousness for themselves, which no man is able to do, or receive it as a gift from the Lord Jesus Christ. How tragic to fall into the way of the Pharisees when the way of life has been provided!

11

Who Is a Murderer?

Matthew 5:21-26

God's requirements for entrance into His presence are no less than the demands of His holiness. When multitudes who had seen the miracles of our Lord pressed upon Him to know what kind of righteousness they must have to enter His presence, He said to them "Except your righteousness shall exceed the righteousness of the scribes and Pharisees, ye shall in no case enter into the kingdom of heaven" (Mt 5:20). The Law of Moses was given to the nation Israel to reveal the holiness of a holy God, and to reveal to them the unholiness of sinful man. It was also given to describe the kind of life a holy God demands of those who would walk in fellowship with Him. The Law was known to these who were pressing the Lord.

But they did not know the requirements of the holiness of God, for they had been schooled in Pharisaic tradition, which said that God is concerned only with the external acts of man. To the Pharisees their God was blind to the thoughts and intents of the heart. In spite of the fact the Old Testament made it very clear that God demands an inward purity as well as outward conformity, the Pharisees had perverted the biblical concept of God, believing their thoughts were unknown to Him and He cared only about their external life. But one who conformed to the outward traditions of the Pharisees would not have that inner righteousness God required for entrance into His presence.

As we enter into this portion of the Sermon on the Mount, beginning at Matthew 5:21, we find a series of paragraphs that contain the statements, "Ye have heard that it was said... but I say unto you." Our Lord purposed to refer to the demands of the Law and show how the Pharisees had misinterpreted and misapplied the Law, and the nation following Pharisaic tradition did not possess a righteousness that qualified them for entrance into the Kingdom of God. It is one thing to say to a man, "You are a sinner," and another thing to demonstrate that fact. So the Lord, step by step, moved through great areas of the Law to show that even though men may have observed the external duties of the Law, they could still be deemed guilty of violating the Law in the sight of God.

Christ began with one of the most obvious violations of the Law. The Law said, "Thou shalt not kill." This was very clear and specific. It is not possible to explain it away. The Pharisees knew what the Law required. Matthew 5:21 said, "Ye have heard that it was said by them of old, Thou shalt not kill; and whosoever shall kill shall be in danger of the judgment." This was a perfectly orthodox statement of the Law concerning the demands of God's holiness. Thou shalt not kill. But the Pharisees interpreted the Law to mean that as long as a man did not plunge a sword into another man's heart, shed his blood, and take his life, he was innocent of breaking the Law and was acceptable to God. To properly interpret what the Law actually demanded, the Lord said, "I say unto you, That whosoever is angry with his brother without a cause shall be in danger of judgment; and whosoever shall say to his brother, Raca, shall be in danger of the council; but whosoever shall say, Thou fool, shall be in danger of hell fire" (v. 22).

The anger, the reproach, and the curse are all external manifestations of an internal attitude of the heart. Our Lord specifically taught that when God said, "Thou shalt not kill," He was not dealing only with the external act but with the attitude which fathers the act. It must have been embarrassing, to those who considered themselves righteous because they had never taken a human life, to have the Lord say to them that in the sight of God there is absolutely no difference between anger and murder. Our Lord said that if one is angry with his brother without a cause he shall be in danger of judgment. This was in contrast to the Pharisees who said, "Whosoever shall kill shall be in danger of judgment" (v. 21). Which meant that no matter what your attitude toward another is, so long as you stop short of actually taking his life, you are not a violator of the Law. The Pharisees considered such a man to be righteous. Our Lord said that one who is angry without cause, even though he does not touch the brother, is in danger of judgment.

Paul said, "Be ye angry, and sin not; let not the sun go down on your wrath" (Eph 4:26). Christians may be angry, and yet, in their anger, not sin. The apostle recognized there is such a thing as righteous indignation, for anger can be the response of injured love. Where love exists, the possibility of anger must exist. Our Lord did not forbid righteous indignation when that which is pure, and righteous, and holy is despised and defiled. Our Lord did say that whosoever is angry with his brother without a cause shall be in danger of the same judgment as though he had actually killed the man.

The word "Raca" was a term of contempt in which one put himself in a superior position and treated his brother with disdain. Our Lord said that when you put yourself in a superior position and speak despitefully of another, you show murder in your heart. Then He proceeded to say that if you call another a fool, you are in danger of hell fire. Such were the demands of the Law of God and the demand of His holiness.

God is revealed in Scripture as a God who loves. He is not only a God who loves, but also He is a God *of* love. He *loves* because He *is* love. When we think of the love of God we turn instinctively to the apostle of love, John. He wrote in 1 John 4:8, "God is love." Because God is love within Himself, He manifests that love by His acts. 1 John 3:16 says, "Hereby perceive we the love of God, because He laid down His life for us: and we ought to lay down our lives for the brethren." 1 John 4:9-10 reads, "In this was manifested the love of God toward us, because that God sent his only begotten Son into the world, that we might live through him. Herein is love, not that we loved God, but that he loved us, and sent his Son to be the propitiation for our sins."

Here is an act that almost defies comprehension. It is not difficult to conceive of God as being a God of love. What is beyond human comprehension is that a holy God could and would love sinners. Paul presented this truth in Romans 5:8-10: "God commended his love toward us, in that, while we were yet sinners, Christ died for us. Much more then, being now justified by his blood, we shall be saved from wrath through him, for if, when we were enemies, we were reconciled to God by the death of his Son, much more, being reconciled, we shall be saved by his life." God is love. Love is His character, and because it is His character, love was willed into action, and God loved His enemies. God loved sinners and sent His beloved Son into the world so that He might die to provide a covering for the sin of sinful men. Scripture impresses upon us that love is a manifestation of God's holiness. God loves because He is holy. The love of God for sinners is a manifestation of His holiness.

Since this is true, any manifestation of hatred or of anger is a manifestation of unholiness. The Lord, who demanded that men conform to the holiness of God to be accepted into His presence, said a man who hates without a cause is manifesting unholiness; therefore, he is disqualified for entrance into the presence of God. May it burn into our consciousness that unjust anger, in the sight of God, is murder, and no murderer has eternal life dwelling in him. Such anger is a manifestation of unholiness.

In Ephesians 3:18-19, Paul prayed that we "may be able to comprehend with all saints what is the breadth, and length, and depth, and height; and to know the love of Christ, which passeth knowledge." The story is told that among the many victims of the French Revolution was a bishop who knew the love of God. He had been committed to prison and awaited execution. One tiny window that admitted light to his dark dungeon was in the form of a cross. After his execution, they found written at the top of that window, "height," and below the window, "depth;" and on either side of that cross, "length" and "breadth." He died knowing that in the cross we enter into the height, and depth, and length, and breadth of the love of God. God's love is a manifestation of God's holiness. Where holiness is and where righteousness is manifest, there is no sinful anger.

Our Lord applied this principle to the life of those concerned about righteousness, holiness, and godliness (Mt 5:23-26). He told the demands this principle makes upon men in two areas: "If thou bring thy gift to the altar, and there rememberest that thy brother hath ought against thee; leave there thy gift before the altar, and go thy way; first be reconciled to thy brother, and then come and offer thy gift" (vv. 23-24). Suppose a man who in obedience to the requirements of the Law comes with his sacrifice to offer it on the altar to God. Is God pleased with that sacrifice? Not necessarily so. For if one is estranged from another, such sacrifice is unacceptable in the sight of God. This one, who professes to be rightly related to God and to manifest his righteousness by obedience to the Law, comes with an offering. As he makes his way toward the altar, his heart is convicted that because of something he has done, his brother is angry with him. The offerer is not angry with the brother; the brother is angry with him because something he has done has offended the brother. The Lord said that before he comes to offer his sacrifice, he is to leave the sacrifice unoffered and settle the matter with his brother. First be reconciled to your brother, then come and offer your gift.

Many of God's children ought to disqualify themselves from fellowship with the saints until first they have removed from an offended brother the anger that is in his heart; only then may they come and offer the sacrifice of praise and thanksgiving.

In the first incident (vv. 23-24) the one who comes with his gift may be innocent. The fault may be entirely with the one who holds the anger against him; but as long as he knows his brother is angry with him, he has no right to come. Even though he may be innocent, God puts the responsibility upon him to rectify the wrong. God does not say to wait until the one who is angry with you comes to make it right. God says that if you know one is out of fellowship with you, you go to him to make it right.

In the second illustration (vv. 25-26) we find one who is guilty. He has done something to offend the brother, so the brother has become his adversary. Christ said, "Agree with thine adversary quickly, whiles thou art in the way with him; lest at any time the adversary deliver thee to the judge, and thou be cast into prison. Verily I say unto thee, Thou shalt by no means come out from thence, till thou hast paid the uttermost farthing" (v. 25). The man is in debt, and because he has been faithless in his obligation, he made the other angry. Our Lord obligated us to remove the cause of the anger lest there be serious complications. In this same vein, Paul wrote in Romans, "Owe no man anything, but to love one another" (14:8). That is the responsibility God places on His children. We are to maintain such a relationship with other members of the body so there is no division. Where there is division there will be anger, and where there is anger, there is no holiness and no godliness, and the demands of God's holiness are not met.

God's standards are as inflexible as God's holiness. If we would walk in fellowship with a holy God, we must conform not only in action but also in thought and in attitude to the holiness of God. This means my life must be subject to the authority of Scripture—not only my external life but also my thought life. If I harbor jealousy, bitterness, anger, malice, wrath against my brother in Christ, I am a murderer in the sight of God. God has revealed His love to capture my heart and to win my heart to Him. As I have been attracted to Him through the love manifested at the cross, I owe Him my love. Giving Him my love, I must love another.

12

God's Moral Standard

Matthew 5:27-32

To prevent shoplifting, one of our large department stores warns, "You are under surveillance by TV." As we turn to the Word of God, we realize we are under the surveillance of God's holiness. God does not simply monitor our outward actions but penetrates deep to reveal what is inside. God knows not only every action but also He knows our thoughts, the intents of our hearts. Perhaps nowhere is that truth more clearly presented than in Matthew 5:27-32, where the Lord laid down God's demands in the realm of moral purity. In a day when premarital and extramarital sex are common, we need to remember that a holy God forbids immorality. God is vitally concerned with the preservation of marriage and of the home. Because it is true that any blessing God has given for the benefit of mankind may be perverted, Scripture has as much to say about the moral realm and its effect on the individual, society, and home, as on any other single sphere of a man's life.

Marriage is not a social institution designed simply for man and therefore devised by man. It is a divine institution. It had its beginning not in society but in the command of God. In the earliest chapters of Genesis, God said, "It is not good that the man should be alone; I will make an help meet for him" (2:18). Marriage had its beginning in the mind of God and was instituted by God. God caused a deep sleep to fall upon Adam; as he slept He took one of his ribs and closed up the flesh. A wife was formed for Adam. "Therefore shall a man leave his father and his mother, and shall cleave unto his wife; and they shall be one flesh" (Gen 2:24). By marriage God joins together a husband and wife in an inseparable, indissoluble union. Two become one flesh. God, as He lays down His commandment concerning marriage protects marriage from violation and also against dissolution.

Marriage was instituted first of all for personal reasons. When God created man and woman, He endowed them with physical appetites. These appetites were God-given and were a blessing bestowed upon mankind. These appetites were given not only for procreation but also for physical and emotional enjoyment. They were a blessing specifically designed by the Creator for the benefit of the creature. This is very clear in Hebrews 13:4, where the apostle wrote that marriage is honorable in all things and the marriage relationship undefiled. In 1 Corinthians, Paul wrote at some length about this and recognizes the physical need of both husband and wife. God provided for this need. "To avoid fornication, let every man have his own wife, and let every woman have her own husband" (7:2). God's solution to the problem of physical desire is not abstinence or control, but marriage. So Paul directed each man to have his own wife and each woman her own husband. In this bond each has a responsibility to the other in the physical realm that Paul outlined so clearly in 1 Corinthians 7:3-5. He recognized the need and showed God's solution.

Marriage was also instituted for social benefits. Society is founded not on the individual but on the family. Lest there be a total disruption of society, God protects marriage as a divine institution so that society may not give way to the corruption which inevitably must come and the dissolution that must result when the smallest unit in society is disrupted.

Not only was marriage designed for personal benefit and for the benefit of society, but also it was designed to be God's object lesson to the world of the relationship existing between a believer and Himself. Because of the entrance of sin into the world, men became strangers to God and foreigners to the intimate relationship established between God and a believer when the two become one. While believers enter into this glorious union with God through Jesus Christ, one outside of Christ knows nothing of this union. God's object lesson to the world of the relationship between a believer and Christ is to be discovered through the relationship between a man and a woman in marriage. God jealously guards His object lesson, which is a means of revealing divine truth to men who are strangers to His truth. Therefore the Lord, recognizing the purpose of marriage in the plan of God, spoke concerning a mistaken concept of marriage.

In the fifth chapter of Matthew our Lord answered the question uppermost in the minds of multitudes who saw Him perform miracles to authenticate Himself to the nation. They wanted to know whether the righteousness learned from the Pharisees was adequate to bring them into relationship with God. Our Lord categorically declared in Matthew 5:20, "Except your righteousness shall exceed the righteousness of the scribes and Pharisees, ye shall in no case enter." Because these people had such respect for the Pharisees and for their system of legal righteousness, they needed an explanation.

Our Lord moved from point to point to show that what the Pharisees taught fell far short of the demands of the unalterable, absolute holiness of God. As He came to the moral realm, He said, "Ye have heard that it was said by them of old time, Thou shalt not commit adultery: but I say unto you, That whosoever looketh on a woman to lust after her hath committed adultery with her already in his heart" (vv. 27-28). The Pharisees were concerned only with outward acts. They acted as though God were ignorant of what was in the mind and heart of a man. But the Lord sought to show that God is concerned not only with what a man is on the outside but also with what he is on the inside. Therefore, in touching on the moral realm, He said that although the Pharisees taught that as long as a man refrains from the physical act of adultery he is acceptable in the sight of God, the truth is that if he has an adulterous heart he is unrighteous, and unholy, and unacceptable in the presence of God. The Pharisees had correctly quoted the commandment given by God to Moses, "Thou shalt not commit adultery" (Ex 20:14). They had deemed it to mean only the outward act. But our Lord went far beyond that.

It was recognized that God hates adultery; the Old Testament made it so very clear. The commandment of Exodus 20:14 was repeated in Leviticus 18:20, "Thou shalt not lie carnally with thy neighbor's wife, to defile thyself with her." In the Old Testament concept, adultery was an immoral act between a man and a married woman. It was a sin against a marriage vow, the marriage contract, the marriage relationship. It was often referred to as a manifestation of covetousness, because the one desiring another's wife was coveting what was not his and to which he had no right. The term was broadened to cover all immorality whether on the part of married or unmarried.

Job spoke of this when he chronicled the sins to which the flesh was heir: In Job 31:9-11 we read, "If mine heart hath been deceived by a woman, or if I have lain wait at my neighbor's door, [he was referring to a custom where men would put a veil over their faces to disguise themselves and then wait for a neighbor's wife] then let my wife grind unto another, and let others bow down upon her. For this is an heinous crime; yea, it is an iniquity to be punished by the judges."

There were few capital crimes under the law, but adultery carried a capital sentence; those taken in adultery were to be put to death. This could be done quickly by thrusting them through with a dart or a sword. It could be performed by strangulation, or it could be punished by the most severe death penalty, stoning.

Israel acknowledged the justice of God's pronouncement. When the Pharisees brought a woman taken in adultery to our Lord (Jn 8), they asked Him if He would concur that this woman ought to be stoned. The nation, through the Old Testament Law, had had burned into its consciousness that a holy God hates immorality to the extent that He demanded a death penalty be carried out by the judges. As Job said, it is "an heinous crime" in the sight of God.

There must have been multitudes there who had not committed the physical act of adultery—had not been guilty of either premarital or extra-marital sex—who sought the Lord's approval and His pronouncement of their acceptability to God. For these He interpreted what the commandment meant. It meant not only that a man was to refrain from the physical act but also to refrain from a lustful glance. For if he looked on a woman with lust, in the sight of God he was as guilty of adultery as though he had committed the act. While the Pharisees said men should not commit a physical act of adultery, they held that as long as they refrained from the physical act they were guiltless in the sight of God. But the Lord said, "But I say unto you, That whosoever looketh on a woman to lust after her hath committed adultery with her already in his heart."

The heart is desperately wicked, and because God-given desires are not brought under control, the mind is often allowed to wander where it will and give itself to adultery. We are subjected on every hand to external stimuli that come unsolicited to our thoughts. A commercial suddenly flashes on the screen. We turn a page in a magazine, and there it is. Fashion is designed to excite and entice. It is not the prostitute on the street that is the only means of solicitation; we are surrounded by it on every hand. God does not say we are excused because of the prevalence of solicitation to evil desires and thoughts. Our Lord said we are responsible for what lodges in our mind. When a lustful thought is permitted to lodge, it becomes adultery in the sight of God.

Job recognized the danger of the thought from an uncontrolled glance. In Job 31:1 he said, "I made a covenant with mine eyes; why then should I think upon a maid?" Again, "If my step hath turned out of the way, and mine heart walked after mine eyes, and if any blot hath cleaved to mine hands; then let me sow, and let another eat" (vv. 7-8). Job recognized that the thought is father to the deed; what he did was the product of what he thought. So Job said, "I made a covenant with mine eyes; why then should I think upon a maid?"

Job had learned the secret our Lord taught His hearers: "If thy right eye offend thee, pluck it out, and cast it from thee: for it is profitable for thee that one of thy members should perish, and not that thy whole body should be cast into hell. And if thy right hand offend thee, cut it off and cast it from thee: for it is profitable for thee that one of thy members should perish, and not that thy whole body should be cast into hell" (Mt 5:29-30). Our Lord was not teaching physical mutilation, for the removal of an eye or amputation of a hand will not change the lustful desire of the heart. A blind man who was a paraplegic could have just as much of a problem with lust as any other individual, and physical mutilation will not solve the problem. What our Lord was saying was to remove the cause, and the cause of adultery is an adulterous heart. The cause of lust is a lustful heart. It is the lustful heart's response to an occasion that produces the act. Go to the root, the old nature within us.

The Lord's words, together with what Job wrote about his experience lest he offend God, ought to bring home to us the danger of an uncontrolled thought life. If we fill ourselves with a playboy philosophy, we can expect to live like a playboy, think like a playboy, and lust like a playboy. We need to be discriminating as to that on which we focus attention. We need control over the mind lest it cater to the lust of the flesh. We need control over the matter of dress lest consciously or unconsciously we solicit lust and incite adultery in the heart of others. The Word speaks again and again about modesty, and in a day of looseness and laxity a word on modesty is more needed than ever.

Our Lord not only safeguarded against the violation of marriage but also He safeguarded against the dissolution of marriage (vv. 31-32). Two become one, by God's law of marriage. One is the smallest indivisible unit. Our Lord instructed that in the sight of God marriage constituted before God was indissoluble. When marriage goes, society goes. When the morals of society have deteriorated, the morals of the individual must suffer. Our Lord made it very clear that in the sight of God only one thing can terminate a marriage, death itself. Paul summarized in Romans 7:1 what he understood our Lord to teach: "Know ye not. . . that the law hath dominion over a man as long as he liveth? For the woman which hath an husband is bound by the law to her husband as long as he liveth; but if the husband be dead, she is loosed from the law of her husband." Paul wrote again, "The wife is bound by the law as long as her husband liveth; but if her husband be dead, she is at liberty to be married to whom she will; only in the Lord" (1 Co 7:39).

The biblical concept, then, is that marriage is an indissoluble union in which two become one in a relationship which in the sight of God can be terminated only by death. This is not an arbitrary thing. It is God's protection not only of the individual, and of the children that spring from that union, but also of society. When the law of God is violated, the individual suffers, society suffers, and—I say it reverently—God suffers.

Malachi 2:14-16 reads, "The LORD hath been witness between thee and the wife of thy youth, against whom thou hast dealt treacherously: yet is she thy companion, and the wife of thy covenant. And did not he make one? . . . For the LORD, the God of Israel, saith that he hateth putting away [divorce]." God hates divorce. Why? Because it affects the individual, because it affects society, and because it totally disrupts the object lesson He has given to the world of the relationship between a believer and Himself.

Society today asks the question, How far can one go? The Word of God is very specific in answering that question. One can go up to the point that desire becomes lust, for lust is adultery. In the light of God's holiness we have to conclude God's standard and the world's standard are diametrically opposed. The world has adopted the standards of man and freely approves premarital and extramarital sex and exchange of wives; and men call that freedom. God calls it the bondage of sin. God's standard is that marriage is inviolable and indissoluble, and the holiness of God demands conformity to His standard not only in act but also in thought and in desire. "Be ye holy; for I am holy" (1 Pe 1:16). That is the requirement of God.

13

The Credibility Gap

Matthew 5:33-37

Our day is characterized by the credibility gap. Every man's word is suspect, and we have adopted the attitude that although we hear what is said, we know what is said is not what is meant. This has become so widespread that government has had to move into the advertising realm and establish certain guidelines about truth in advertising. Facts we had accepted as truth are now found to be false. So we have come to mistrust almost everything that is said. In the light of this, our Lord's word as He described characteristics of a righteous man are relevant.

> Ye have heard that it hath been said by them of old time, Thou shalt not forswear thyself [perjure yourself or break your oath], but shalt perform unto the Lord thine oaths: but I say unto you, Swear not at all; neither by heaven; for it is God's throne: nor by the earth; for it is his footstool: neither by Jerusalem; for it is the city of the great King. Neither shalt thou swear by thy head, because thou canst not make one hair white or black. But let your communication be, Yea, yea; Nay, nay: for whatsoever is more than these cometh of evil (Mt 5:33-37).

The practice of taking an oath has roots very deep in the Old Testament. A man took an oath to affirm the truth of the words he spoke. The oath was a curse he placed on himself if his word were not true or his promise not fulfilled.

This is illustrated clearly in the familiar experience in Peter's life (Mt 26:69-75). After Jesus' arrest, a damsel at the gate said to Peter, "Thou also wast with Jesus of Galilee. But he [Peter] denied before them all" (vv. 69-70). Peter first denied by saying, "I know not what thou sayest" (v. 70).

When he went to the porch, another maid saw him and said to those who were there, "This fellow was also with Jesus of Nazareth. And again he denied with an oath, I do not know the man" (vv. 71-72). In the second step, Peter made a statement and he supported the statement by calling someone or something to witness to the truth of his word. A man would take an oath because the Law said that by the mouth of two witnesses a matter would be established (Deu 19:15). When a man made an affirmation himself, his word could be suspect. But when he called another to witness his word, his word was established as truth. So Peter confirmed his word with an oath.

But then, "After a while came unto him they that stood by, and said to Peter, Surely thou also art one of them; for thy speech bewrayeth thee. Then began he to curse and to swear, saying, I know not the man" (Mt 26:73-74). Peter was not violating the commandment that said, "Thou shalt not take the name of the LORD thy God in vain" (Ex 20:7) when he cursed. He was progressing to a third stage in affirming the truth of his word. After he had made a statement and had called someone or something to witness his statement, he put himself under a curse if the word he had spoken and affirmed by an oath were not true. So Peter had made a statement, and then he had taken an oath; then he had put himself under a curse affirming the truth of his word.

It is this idea our Lord had in mind when he referred to the custom of the Jews in our Lord's day who took oaths or put curses upon themselves. The Pharisees read the Law and understood it to mean, "Thou shalt not be guilty of perjury; thou shalt not put yourself under an oath affirming as truth that which you know to be false. Nor shall you put yourself under a curse to do that which you know to be untrue." Such was their interpretation of the Law.

In 2 Samuel 19 King David did this very thing. "Therefore the king said unto Shimei, Thou shalt not die. And the king sware unto him" (v. 23). Now that was a promise, a pledge David made. The king who gave his word, "Thou shalt not die," put himself under a curse to show he intended to fulfil what he had promised. It was Old Testament custom and was acceptable.

In Exodus 22 this curse or oath was used in connection with matters of Law. When there was a case of adjudication between two individuals, it was customary for them to put themselves under an oath or a curse. "If a man deliver unto his neighbour an ass, or an ox, or a sheep, or any beast, to keep; and it die, or be hurt, or driven away, no man seeing it: then shall an oath of the LORD be between them both, that he hath not put his hand unto his neighbour's goods; and the owner of it shall accept thereof, and he shall not make it good" (Ex 22:10-11). Here is a matter that might have ended in a lawsuit. Suppose man had entrusted the oversight of his flock to another and something happened to one of the sheep. The overseer could take an oath that he had been careful in fulfilling his responsibility and it was not his fault the sheep had wandered away. If the man affirmed his word with an oath, that would end the matter, and there could be no litigation.

This was common not only in matters of law but also in daily life. When Abraham sent his trusted servant to find a bride for Isaac, he made the servant pledge he would not take as Isaac's wife a daughter of the heathen around him. "Abraham said unto his eldest servant of his house, that ruled over all that he had, Put, I pray thee, thy hand under my thigh: And I will make thee swear by the LORD, the God of heaven, and the God of the earth" (Gen 24:2-3). He was to put his hand on the thigh because it is the most powerful muscle in the body. They were swearing by the strength of the individual, which signified that all of his power and all of his might would go into fulfilling his word.

These incidents show that the Mosaic Law permitted oaths. They were a part of daily commerce. They were a means to enter into a binding agreement. They were the means to settle matters without going to court. The Law permitted these oaths; in fact, in many instances the oaths were required. They were used as legal contracts. When a man appeared before a judge and took an oath, it was the same as having a legal document notarized today. It was binding upon the participants in the contract.

There were a number of different ways men took oaths. According to 1 Samuel 1:26 they could swear by the life of a person. Someone other than the one making an affirmation was a witness to his words. In 1 Samuel 17:55 men swore by the life of the king. The king was not personally present, but they used the exalted name of the king to be a witness to what they promised.

Matthew 23:16 speaks of men swearing by the Temple, because the Temple was the center of the religious life of Israel. The same passage refers to swearing by the gold that was part of the Temple. Men selected one part of the Temple and called that to bear witness to their words. The idea was that if their word were not true, they would give you the Temple, or the gold that adorns the Temple as your possession.

In the passage before us in Matthew 5, Jesus referred to those who swore by heaven (v. 34), or by earth (v. 35), or by the city of Jerusalem itself (v. 35). One of the commonest methods of taking an oath was to lift the hand to heaven and swear by the God of heaven. That idea survives in our courts of law today, for a man is asked to raise his right hand and solemnly swear. That method is referred to in the Old Testament as far back as Genesis. In Genesis 14:22-23, "Abram said to the king of Sodom, I have lift up mine hand unto the LORD, the most high God, the possessor of heaven and earth, that I will not take from a thread even to a shoelatchet, and that I will not take any thing that is thine, lest thou shouldest say, I have made Abram rich." He entered into an oath by lifting up his hand unto heaven.

In Genesis 31:50 we read the words of Jacob: "God is witness betwixt me and thee." Jacob was calling God to witness the truth of his word. It was a formula for taking an oath. In Judges 8:9 the formula used is, "As Jehovah liveth." This affirmed the truth by the fact that God lives, meaning that a man's word was as permanent as God's life. Jeremiah said, "The LORD be a true and faithful witness between us" (42:5). These formulas were used to affirm an oath and assure the truth of a statement.

When we come to the New Testament, we find the New Testament does not forbid taking oaths. In 2 Corinthians 1:23, Paul took an oath. "I call God for a record upon my soul, that to spare you I came not as yet unto Corinth." Paul used an Old Testament formula that meant God was his witness.

Matthew 26:63-64 records that when Jesus was questioned before Caiaphas, He "held his peace. And the high priest answered and said unto him, I adjure thee by the living God, that thou tell us whether thou be the Christ, the Son of God." The high priest put Christ under an oath when he said, "I adjure thee by the living God." He meant, "as God is your witness, tell me the truth."

Jesus saith unto him, Thou hast said," or, "It is true; I confess it." So Jesus Christ Himself was under an oath, and He took an oath.

It is significant also that the Book of Hebrews refers to God affirming His word with an oath. "When God made promise to Abraham [and the promise was a spoken word], because he could swear by no greater, he sware by himself, saying, Surely blessing I will bless thee, and multiplying I will multiply thee" (6:13-14). The writer to the Hebrews said when God gave His word to Abraham He affirmed the word with an oath.

Thus, in the New Testament, Paul put himself under an oath; Jesus Christ was put under an oath, and He answered under oath; and God Himself is said to have ratified His word to Abraham by putting Himself under oath.

With that background, look at the Lord's words as He dealt with this matter of oaths. The rabbis taught, "Thou shalt not forswear thyself, but shalt perform unto the Lord thine oaths" (Mt 5:33). What you have promised and ratified by an oath you are obligated to fulfill. That would be an acceptable summary of Old Testament teaching on this matter of oaths. "But I say unto you, Swear not at all;

neither by heaven; for it is God's throne: nor by the earth; for it is his footstool: neither by Jerusalem; for it is the city of the great King. Neither shalt thou swear by thy head [offering your life as a payment if your word is not true]" (Mt 5:34-36). What we discover in this passage is that, while the Old Testament allowed oaths to legalize a pledge between two men, oaths had become necessary because men were such deceivers and liars. What was begun as a legal contract now had become absolutely necessary because of duplicity, because of the lack of regard for truth. No man's word was considered true; all men were deemed to be lying.

Since Christ allowed Himself to be put under oath (Mt 26:63-64), we conclude He was not here saying, "Do not consent to be put under an oath." He was saying, "Let your character, your reputation for honesty, your word be so obviously true and undefiled and without duplicity, that no man would think it necessary to put you under an oath because he suspects you of deception." Instead of the duplicity, "let your communication be Yea, yea; Nay, nay." Some words can have a double meaning, and some words can be interpreted in two different ways. But there is only one possible way of interpreting yes. Yes does not mean "no." There is only one way you can interpret no. You can never interpret that as meaning consent. When you say yes, it means yes; when you say no, it means no. The Lord demanded that one's speech be so trustworthy that men would not have to debate what was meant and interpret what was said. They would know what was meant because he was an honest man.

James, throughout his epistle, commented on what our Lord taught concerning the life of righteousness in the Sermon on the Mount. What our Lord taught in Matthew 5:33-37 James stated this way: "The tongue is a little member [i.e., in comparison with other organs of the body], and boasteth great things. Behold, how great a matter a little fire kindleth! And the tongue is a fire, a world of iniquity: so is the tongue among our members, that it defileth the whole body, and setteth on fire the course of

nature; and it is set on fire of hell" (Ja 3:5-6). The first
description James gave of the tongue was that it is a destructive evil. It can create as much devastation as one
match in the dry leaves of a forest floor. It is devastating
and destructive.

The second thing he said about the tongue is, "Every
kind of beasts, and of birds, and of serpents, and of things
in the sea, is tamed, and hath been tamed of mankind: but
the tongue can no man tame" (v. 7). It is untamable and
uncontrollable.

The third thing he said about the tongue is, "It is an
unruly evil, full of deadly poison" (v. 8). It is evil.

The fourth description is that it is inconsistent. There is
an inconsistency in the tongue of man never found in any
other part of God's creation. Of all creation, the mouth is
the only place this inconsistency is found. "Therewith
bless we God, even the Father; and therewith curse we
men, which are made after the similitude of God. Out of the
same mouth proceedeth blessing and cursing. My brethren, these things ought not so to be. Doth a fountain send
forth at the same place sweet water and bitter? Can the fig
tree, my brethren, bear olive berries? either a vine, figs? so
can no fountain both yield salt water and fresh" (vv. 9-12).

Because the tongue is destructive, untamable, evil, and
inconsistent, our Lord said, "Let your speech be so without
deception and duplicity that men will be able to accept as
truth what you say."

A story has come down in my family and was given to
me as a pattern for life when I was just a lad. My great
grandfather had twelve children. Two of those served in
the Union Army in the Civil War and were captured by the
Confederate Army and confined in Andersonville Prison
in Richmond, Virginia. They had been there for an extended period of time when my great grandfather decided
to visit his sons. To visit them he had to get a permit to pass
through the lines. He knew the Secretary of State who
served under President Lincoln, and obtained a letter from
him to permit him to pass through the lines. The letter
read, "This is to introduce to you one whose word is as

good as his bond, and his bond as the Bank of England."
My great grandfather hardly had two coins to rattle together in his pocket. It was not the money he passed down
to the family in which the family took pride, but the fact his
word was as good as his bond.

Righteousness demands absolute truth. Righteousness
does not have a double standard, and a man's daily speech
is to be as trustworthy as his oath. God said we were to
control our speech so that an oath would not be necessary.
Let your yea be yea and your nay be nay to manifest the
righteousness of Christ.

14

An Eye for an Eye

Matthew 5:38-42

Our day is characterized by lawlessness. It has permeated our society to an unanticipated and unprecedented degree. Those whose profession is the law are being called upon to rethink the purpose of law in society. In our day the individual demands his own rights, and demands the right to do as he pleases. The effect it may have on someone else's life is given little consideration.

The Word of God is very specific about the purpose of law. Whether it is the law of government in society; or law in the home; or law in church; or the law of God given through Moses, or the principles and commandments of grace that came from the lips of the Lord Jesus—all law has the same primary purpose. It is to protect innocent people from lawless men. Paul wrote,

> The law is not made for a righteous man, but for the lawless and disobedient, for the ungodly and for sinners, for unholy and profane, for murderers of fathers and murderers of mothers, for manslayers, for whoremongers, for them that defile themselves with mankind, for menstealers, for liars, for perjured persons, and if there be any other thing that is contrary to sound doctrine; according to the glorious gospel of the blessed God, which was committed to my trust (1 Ti 1:9-11).

In that succinct statement the apostle taught that God gave law for the protection of righteous men against ungodly men, and for the protection of the innocent from the unrighteous.

When our Lord, in Matthew 5, outlined for men the requirements of godliness and holiness and righteousness, He made a statement that has puzzled many. It is a proverb which is little understood. Our Lord, referring to the law of the Old Testament, said,

> Ye have heard that it hath been said, An eye for an eye, and a tooth for a tooth: but I say unto you, That ye resist not evil: but whosoever shall smite thee on thy right cheek, turn to him the other also. And if a man will sue thee at the law, and take away thy coat, let him have thy cloke also. And whosoever shall compel thee to go a mile, go with him twain. Give to him that asketh thee, and from him that would borrow of thee turn not thou away (5:38-42).

The Lord dealt here with the basic problems of why the Law was given, what use the believer should make of the Law, and how a righteous man can use the Law.

Three times the Old Testament stated what the Lord quotes in Matthew 5:38, "An eye for an eye, and a tooth for a tooth." Look into the Old Testament to see how that principle was stated and used. Turn first to Exodus:

> If men strive, and hurt a woman with child, so that her fruit depart from her, and yet no mischief follow: he shall be surely punished, according as the woman's husband shall lay upon him; and he shall pay as the judges determine. And if any mischief follow, then thou shalt give life for life, eye for eye, tooth for tooth, hand for hand, foot for foot, burning for burning, wound for wound, stripe for stripe. If a man smite the eye of his servant, or the eye of his maid, that it perish; he shall let him go free for his eye's sake. And if he smite out his manservant's tooth, or his maidservant's tooth; he shall let him go free for his tooth's sake (Ex 21:22-29).

In this passage God wrote into the Law the principle that for damage inflicted there must be a repayment of equal value. If a man smote a pregnant woman so she lost the child she carried, the husband had the right to determine the value of the child to him, and the one who injured the mother-to-be was responsible to pay equal value. If a man did a person harm, resulting in the loss of eyesight, or the loss of hand or foot, judges had to determine the value of the loss, and there had to be repayment of equal value. A token repayment would not suffice; the demands of justice are not satisfied by a mere token repayment. There had to be repayment of equal value for the injury done.

The second instance where this phrase is used is Leviticus 24:19-20: "If a man cause a blemish in his neighbour; as he has done, so shall it be done to him; breach for breach, eye for eye, tooth for tooth: as he hath caused a blemish in a man, so shall it be done to him again." God did not require mutilation of the party who caused the injury. But He did say that there had to be a payment of equal value, determined by the individual who was injured. The Law protected the innocent from the guilty and required there should be a repayment of equal value for injury done. It was the right of the injured party to expect repayment; It was not the one inflicting the injury who had rights to be protected. It was the one who was injured who had rights that were to be defended and protected by Law. Under the Law of God, the one who was unrighteous or who violated the Law lost his rights. It was the one injured who had rights, and the Law protected those rights from the one inflicting the injury.

Another use of this principle is in Deuteronomy 19:15-21. Here there is a second provision of protection for an innocent man. This was not protection from injury; that had already been covered in Exodus and Leviticus. This was protection from a false accusation.

> One witness shall not rise up against a man for any iniquity, or for any sin, in any sin that he sinneth: at the mouth of two witnesses, or at the mouth of three witnesses, shall the matter be established. If a false witness rise up against any man to testify against him that which is wrong; then both the men, between whom the controversy is, shall stand before the LORD, before the priests and the judges, which shall be in those days; and the judges shall make diligent inquisition: and, behold, if a witness be a false witness, and hath testified falsely against his brother; then shall he do unto him, as he had thought to have done unto

his brother: so shalt thou put the evil away from among you. And those which remain shall hear, and fear, and shall henceforth commit no more any such evil among you. And thine eye shall not pity; but life shall go for life, eye for eye, tooth for tooth, hand for hand, foot for foot.

What this passage says is that, if two men agreed they were going to lodge a false accusation against an individual to collect from him something not rightfully theirs, and the judges find these men are false witnesses, what they were trying to get out of the innocent man, they would have to pay to him for damages from the false accusation. They had to pay him equal to what they were trying to extort from him, eye for eye, tooth for tooth; equal retribution or repayment for a false accusation.

From these three references we see that God protected the innocent from the guilty. In all of these instances the innocent had rights and could demand them, and it was perfectly just before the Law to demand them. Why, then, did Christ say, "Ye have heard that it hath been said, An eye for an eye, and a tooth for a tooth: but I say unto you, That ye resist not evil: but whosoever shall smite thee on thy right cheek, turn to him the other also" (Mt 5:38-39)? What Christ said is that while a righteous man may have his rights, a righteous man will evidence his righteousness by giving up his rights.

Righteousness, godliness, and holiness, do not demand their rights. It is the character of righteousness and godliness to give up rights. Jesus Christ became the supreme example of this, for He stood before Pilate charged with false, unsupported accusations. He had the right to demand repayment for the false accusation, but He also had the right to give up His rights. He manifested His godliness and holiness not by demanding what was rightfully His but by giving up what was His. When these people flocked to our Lord to ask, "What marks a righteous man?" the Lord Jesus said, "A righteous man is characterized by a selflessness that does not demand one's own right."

This selflessness is a manifestation of love, for a primary

characteristic of love is that it is considerate. Love does not seek its own good; it seeks the good of its object. The Lord taught that if a man does you wrong—smites you on one cheek—you should not respond by demanding your rights to repayment. You should forego your rights, even if he presumes upon your love and selflessness and smites you a second time. Christ said this is what characterizes righteousness. If he sues you for your coat, you give him your coat; if he goes beyond what he had a right to demand, and extracts from you further than his due, you do not stand for your rights. You give up your rights to demonstrate the righteousness of Christ.

The land of Palestine was occupied territory in our Lord's day. Israel was overrun with Roman soldiers. Soldiers must move from place to place. The method of transporting the goods of a soldier was to conscript men who would carry their burdens for them. When a Roman soldier moved from one village to the next, he would take some able-bodied man from the village and compel him to carry his things to the next village. To protect those who lived in occupied territory from the Roman soldier's right to requisition burden-bearers, the Roman law said the soldier could conscript a civilian to carry his burden for only one mile. Then the man was to be released and the soldier would have to find someone else or carry the burden himself. Our Lord said that, if someone conscripted you to carry his burden the required mile and you came to the end of the mile and the soldier released you, you should gladly carry it further. The conscripted one had his rights. They were protected by law, but he had the right to give up his rights to manifest the righteousness of Christ.

This principle permeates the New Testament and comes into the writings of Paul. "Let love be without dissimulation [hypocrisy]. Abhor that which is evil; cleave to that which is good. Be kindly affectioned one to another with brotherly love; in honour preferring one another" (Ro 12:9-10). A righteous man manifests love. Love is considerate and selfless. How will that love work itself out? Paul said, "Bless them which persecute you: bless, and curse not. Rejoice with them that do rejoice, and weep with them that weep" (vv. 14-15). "Dearly beloved, avenge not yourselves [don't stand on your own rights, don't demand your just due], but rather give place unto wrath: for it is written, Vengeance is mine; I will repay, saith the Lord" (v. 19). If a wrong has been done, turn it over to the Lord. Do not retaliate, do not seek your own rights. "If thine enemy hunger, feed him; if he thirst, give him drink: for in so doing thou shalt heap coals of fire on his head. Be not overcome of evil, but overcome evil with good" (vv. 20-21). Paul showed us what our Lord said in Matthew 5: You have rights. Your rights have been injured. You have a right to demand some retribution. But the righteous man leaves that to God, and he manifests love and forgiveness, even to his enemies. That is righteousness in action.

Paul referred to this same principle again in 1 Corinthians 6. Here he wrestled with the problem of a believer going to law against another believer to collect what is rightfully his. One man stood on his own rights, and the apostle criticized the discrediting his testimony before an unbelieving world (v. 7): "Why do you not rather take wrong? why do ye not rather suffer yourselves to be defrauded?" Paul said the mark of a godly man is that he gives up his rights so he might manifest the selfless love of Christ.

Romans 13:10 says, "Love worketh no ill to his neighbour: therefore love is the fulfilling of the law." The Law gives us rights, but also gives us the liberty to forego our rights so that we might show the righteousness of Christ. We have our rights; our rights are protected by the Word of God. But we also have liberty to forego our rights to manifest the love of Christ. It is not the demanding of his rights that marks a righteous man—but the giving up of his rights that characterizes the man who pleases God.

15

Love Your Enemy

Matthew 5:43-48

A missionary from the islands told of an old Maori woman who had won the name Warrior Brown because of her fighting qualities. Warrior Brown had been converted, and her life was changed. On one occasion she was giving her testimony to a group gathered in her old haunts of sin, when someone threw a potato and struck her. The people who had known her expected to see an explosion from Warrior Brown. Instead she stooped down, picked up the potato, and put it in the pocket of her apron. When she concluded her testimony, she went home. Some time passed, and it came time for the fall thanksgiving service. It was the custom of the believers to bring some of the fruits of their labors to give to the Lord at the harvest festival. Warrior Brown brought a sack of potatoes. When they asked her about her offering, she told them she had taken the potato thrown at her that day and had cut it up and planted it, and she was giving the Lord the fruits of the increase.

Our Lord electrified the crowd standing around Him as He addressed Himself to the question, How good does a man have to be to please God? He said to them, "Love your enemies." In this climactic statement, in which our Lord showed the products of righteousness in a man's life, He conveyed a concept unheard of to those who followed the Pharisees.

The Pharisees taught that it was the responsibility of a righteous man to love. After all, that fact was inescapable

in the Old Testament. Since God is love, and righteousness
is a manifestation of the nature of God in God's child,
God's child must manifest before men what belongs to his
heavenly Father. But the concept of loving an enemy
seemed to go contrary to all Old Testament teaching. Yet
our Lord taught, "Ye have heard that it hath been said,
Thou shalt love thy neighbor, and hate thine enemy. But I
say unto you, Love your enemies, bless them that curse
you, do good to them that hate you, and pray for them
which despitefully use you, and persecute you; that ye
may be the children of your Father which is in heaven" (Mt
5:43-45).

The principle of loving your friends and hating your
enemies certainly had Old Testament precedent: "Thou
shalt not avenge, nor bear any grudge against the children
of thy people, but thou shalt love thy neighbor as thyself: I
am the LORD" (Lev 19:18).

In the Commandments, the Israelites were commanded
to love those who were their neighbors. In this passage,
"neighbor" meant anyone who was a member of the com-
monwealth of Israel. They were strictly forbidden to
avenge or to harbor a grudge against the children of their
people, but, conversely, they were commanded. "Thou
shalt love thy neighbor as thyself." But the children of
Israel formed one small segment of the population of the
earth. They, by the Law of God, had been separated from all
other peoples. They were forbidden to behave as the others
behaved, to dress as the other dressed, to eat as the others
ate, to marry outside of the nation. God desired to keep
them a people set apart for His own use. The Law demanded that those within the fellowship and family
should have a family love for one another.

But the Law said nothing about their responsibility to
those who were outside. In fact, there were occasions
when they were forbidden to love those who were outside
the family:

> An Ammonite or Moabite shall not enter into the congrega-
> tion of the LORD: even to their tenth generation shall they
> not enter into the congregation of the LORD for ever. Be-

cause they met you not with bread and with water in the
way, when ye came forth out of Egypt; and because they
hired against thee Balaam the son of Beor of Pethor of
Mesopotamia, to curse thee. Nevertheless the LORD thy God
would not hearken unto Balaam; but the LORD thy God
turned the curse into a blessing unto thee, because the LORD
thy God loved thee. Thou shalt not seek their peace nor
their prosperity all thy days for ever (Deu 23:3-6).

We discover from Genesis 19:33-38 that the children of
Ammon and the children of Moab were descendants of
Lot, born from the incestuous relationship between Lot
and his two daughters while he was intoxicated. The
Moabites and the Ammonites were blood relatives of the
Israelites. When God redeemed the children of Israel out of
Egypt and sent them on their journey through the wilderness to the promised land, these blood relatives opposed
Israel's entrance into the land. Here were a traveling people who desired to purchase food and water from the
people through whose lands they passed. But the Ammonites and the Moabites refused to sell Israelites water or
food. They were sinning against blood. God said that because the Ammonites and Moabites became the enemies of
Israel, they would never be acceptable in the nation. They
could partake of none of the blessings God would provide
for Abraham's children. Deuteronomy 23 carries the divine command that, while they were to love their neighbor, there were certain enemies they were to hate forever
and to exclude from fellowship and participation in their
blessings.

The Pharisees knew the Old Testament and had de-
duced their principles of righteousness by superimposing
these two commandments. They taught that godliness re-
quires that one love those who are lovely, those near and
dear to you; but one is justified in hating anyone else. The
Lord, as He gave instruction concerning righteousness,
moved beyond the requirement of the Pharisees and said
that, while the Pharisees had correctly said they were to
hate their enemy, He commanded them to love their
enemy, to bless them that cursed them, to do good to them

that hated them, and to pray for them which despitefully used them and persecuted them.

The children of Israel, as they hated those who opposed the will of God, were revealing the justice of God. But the Lord designed that those who manifested righteousness should be instruments—not to reveal the justice of God by hating those who oppose Him—but to reveal the love of God even though they do oppose Him. God's love was not given only to those who respond; it was given to the whole world. "For God so loved the world, that he gave his only begotten Son, that whosoever believeth in him should not perish, but have everlasting life" (Jn 3:16). While Israel, by excluding the Ammonites and the Moabites, became an instrument to reveal the justice of God, God prepared a people who would be instruments to reveal the fathomless love of God that goes beyond any length, or breadth, or height, or depth of understanding. Therefore, Christ said, if you would prove yourself to be a child of God, then you must love as God loved.

God's love is not discriminatory. Nor is it selective. Our Lord emphasized that in Matthew 5:45 when He said, God "maketh his sun to rise on the evil and on the good, and he sendeth rain on the just and on the unjust." Sun and rain are representative of all the blessings that come to men from the hand of God. But God does not send cloudy weather to the unjust and cause the sun to shine on his just neighbor. God does not send rain to one man's field and deny it to the field next door because the man is unjust. When God sends His blessings, they are showered upon the whole earth, whether men are just or unjust. Such is the nature of God's love.

When God ultimately provided the blessing of salvation for sinners, it was provided for all men, for Jesus Christ became, "the propitiation for our sins: and not for ours only [who believe], but also for the sins of the whole world (1 Jn 2:2). While all the world does not reap the benefit of salvation, Christ died for the sins of the world. Such was the love of God, that salvation was showered upon the just and the unjust. If a man is discriminatory in his affections, he does not manifest the love of God, which is without bounds.

When the Lord spoke of the love of God, He was not speaking in the context of emotions, but in the context of the will. While all men may not cause an emotional response within us, yet we can will to meet those needs that we know. The love of God is a love of the will; it recognizes the needs of the object of His affection, and moves His mighty hands to meet the need. When one sees another in need and, apart from or in spite of emotions, does something about that need, he is loving as God loves. To love your enemies means to seek the good or the benefit of your enemies.

Paul had this in mind in, "The love of Christ constraineth us" (2 Co 5:14). He was a Hebrew of the Hebrews. He was taught all of the prejudices of the Hebrews against Gentiles, and to Hebrews the Gentiles were an unclean and detestable people. A Hebrew who came in contact with a Gentile was ceremonially unclean; therefore, in obedience to their law, they avoided any contact with Gentiles. But God, in the mystery of His will, reached down to this Hebrew of the Hebrews, and appointed him His representative to bring the Gospel to the Gentiles. Paul submitted to the will of the Lord. Did Paul immediately lose all of his old prejudices and fears? Did Gentiles suddenly become attractive to him? Not for a moment. Gentiles did not bring an emotional response in the heart of the apostle, but Paul could be concerned about their welfare. So he gave himself to preach the Gospel to the Gentiles without reservation. He was motivated by the love of Christ and sought the good of the Gentiles.

Why does a missionary leave the conveniences and companionship of this country and go to a foreign shore? Because those people elicit an emotional response in his heart? No, that is impossible. But because he is concerned about their welfare, and realizes their lostness, and wants to bring a message of salvation to those who have never heard. In being concerned with their good, he manifests the love of God for those who may be naturally unattractive and unlovely.

Would you prove before the world you are a child of God? Our Lord says prove it by your care and concern for one with whom there are no emotional ties. Take one outside the family circle or your circle of friends or perhaps even your circle of acquaintances. Love your enemies. To respond to the needs of those who are in your family is to show natural affection. The natural man loves his wife and his children, seeks their welfare, provides for their needs. Such is natural affection. To love those who are in the family of God is only to display a natural affection. To go beyond the bounds of those with whom we are one, and have concern for those who are outside of the family is to display a supernatural affection. Our Lord calls for this in Matthew 5:46-48. "If ye love them which love you, what reward have ye? do not even the publicans the same? And if ye salute your brethren only [i.e., fellowship with those to whom you have natural ties], what do you more than others? do not even the publicans so? Be ye therefore perfect, even as your Father which is in heaven is perfect."

Now we move into a summary statement where our Lord answers the question uppermost in the minds of His hearers, How good does a man have to be to please God? Christ's answer was, "As good as God is." God is not satisfied with anything less than absolute perfection. How good does a man have to be to stand in the presence of God? He has to be as good as God is. If one falls the slightest degree short of the standard of God's inviolable, unalterable holiness, he is unacceptable to God. What is God's standard? "Be ye therefore as perfect as your Father in heaven is perfect."

If you think back through Matthew 5, you recall the Lord has touched several areas of a man's life. God does not hate; therefore, if a man is as perfect as God is, he will not hate (vv. 21-26). God does not lust; if a man is as perfect as God is, he will not lust (vv. 27-32). God does not deceive; if a man is as perfect as God is, he will not deceive (vv.

33-37). God does not retaliate for injury done; if a man is as perfect as God is, he will not retaliate. He will not stand on his own rights (vv. 39-42). God does not discriminate in His response to needs; if a man is perfect, he will love not only his friends but also his enemies (vv. 43-47). These are the marks of a truly godly man.

What is righteousness? Righteousness is the character of God reproduced in the child of God. What is godliness? The conduct of God reproduced in a child of God. Anything unbecoming to the holiness of God is unbecoming in the life of the child of God. Hatred, lust, deceit, insistence on one's own rights, and a discriminating love are not marks of godliness. They are marks of a natural man.

Peter, one who heard our Lord speak on this occasion, wrote, "As he which hath called you is holy, so be ye holy in all manner of conversation; because it is written: Be ye holy; for I am holy," (1 Pe 1:15-16). God has put before His children impossibly high demands, but because they are unattainable by the flesh God has not lowered His standards. The Lord still says, "Be ye therefore perfect, even as your Father which is in heaven is perfect."

This portion of the Lord's teaching emphasizes that God has called us to holiness—a word that has largely dropped out of our vocabulary. Nevertheless, it is the standard of conduct for the child of God, as the Lord's words in Matthew 5:20 clearly show.

16

Sounding Your Own Trumpet

Matthew 6:1-4

The multitudes who came to hear the Lord teach had been taught a system of righteousness propagated by the Pharisees. He showed them that what the Pharisees interpreted as righteousness was not righteousness at all, for they were content to give external obedience to the Law without the obedience of the heart. We discovered from Matthew 5 that Pharisaic observance of the external law would not make one righteous in the sight of God.

Not only was the Pharisees' interpretation of the Law erroneous, but also the Pharisees' practice of the Law was erroneous. As we move into Matthew 6 in our study of the Sermon on the Mount, we find our Lord had to repudiate the Pharisees' practice of giving alms, their practice of prayer and of fasting, and their attitude toward riches.

The Lord said,

> Take heed that ye do not your alms before men, to be seen of them: otherwise ye have no reward of your Father which is in heaven. Therefore when thou doest thine alms, do not sound a trumpet before thee, as the hypocrites do in the synagogues and in the streets, that they may have glory of men. Verily I say unto you, They have their reward. But when thou doest alms, let not thy left hand know what thy right hand doeth: that thine alms may be in secret: and thy Father which seeth in secret himself shall reward thee openly (Mt 6:1-4).

The fruit of a righteous heart is righteous acts. The foremost fruit of righteousness is love. Paul taught, "Now abideth faith, hope and love, but the greatest of these is love" (1 Co 13:13). In answering the lawyer's questions in Luke 10, the Lord again bore this out: "A certain lawyer [one skilled in the interpretation of the Mosaic Law] stood up, and tempted him, saying, Master, what shall I do to inherit eternal life? He said unto him, What is written in the law? how readest thou? And he answering said, Thou shalt love the Lord thy God with all thy heart, and with all thy soul, and with all thy strength, and with all thy mind; and thy neighbor as thyself" (vv. 25-27). Love is the foremost product of righteousness, and it is what God looks for in a man's life as evidence he has been justified.

This was not only a principle of the Law, but also Paul testified to the same truth: "The end [goal in view] of the commandment is charity [love] out of a pure heart, and of a good conscience, and of faith unfeigned" (1 Ti 1:5). Thus, love is an evidence of righteousness. Paul, looking back to the fruit of righteousness in the Old Testament, testified that love is a fruit of righteousness to satisfy God according to the demands of the Law.

John said, "My little children, let us not love in word, neither in tongue; but in deed and in truth" (1 Jn 3:18). "Beloved, let us love one another: for love is of God; and everyone that loveth is born of God, and knoweth God. He that loveth not knoweth not God; for God is love" (1 Jn 4:7-8). "Beloved, if God so loved us, we ought also to love one another" (1 Jn 4:11).

Love is primarily a care and a concern for the needs of the object of one's affection. The love which satisfies the heart of God is not an emotional response to one who is attractive. The love that satisfies the heart of God is a response to the need of another individual, no matter how unattractive he may be to us. John asked, he that "hath this world's good, and seeth his brother have need, and shutteth up his bowels of compassion from him, how dwelleth the love of God in him?" (1 Jn 3:17). The nature of God is to love. His nature compelled Him to give even though those to whom He gave were unattractive in His sight because they were sinners. This type of love is the test throughout the Word of God as to whether a man loves as God expects him to in order to demonstrate his righteousness before God. Love is a response to a man's need.

This was so evident that in the Old Testament the Jews thought giving alms was the foremost fruit of righteousness. To the Jews, of all of the virtuous actions that would spring from a righteous heart, giving of alms to one in need was primary. This was a matter of record in the Law, for Deuteronomy 15:9 reads, "Beware that there be not a thought in thy wicked heart, saying, The seventh year, the year of release, is at hand; and thine eye be evil against thy poor brother, and thou givest him nought; and he cry unto the LORD against thee, and it be sin unto thee." Moses said that not to give when a brother's need is known is sin before God. "Thou shalt surely give him, and thine heart shall not be grieved when thou givest unto him: because that for this thing the LORD thy God shall bless thee in all thy works, and in all thou puttest thine hand unto. For the poor shall never cease out of the land: therefore I command thee, saying, thou shalt open thy hand wide unto thy brother, to thy poor, to thy needy, in thy land" (vv. 10-11). The Law made it very specific that to see a brother in need and not respond was a sin against God; further, when you gave you were not to give grudgingly as though it had been extracted from you and you expected to suffer the same way you would if a tooth had been extracted; but you were to give joyfully and gladly. Thus, God would bless the giver. This was so fundamental in the Law as a manifestation of righteousness that the Jews had focused attention upon this requirement and had made it the primary evidence of righteousness of the Law.

The Pharisees had gone far beyond any legitimate interpretation of this passage in Deuteronomy. The people had been told: "Lay up alms in thy storehouse, it shall deliver thee from affliction." "Alms delivers from death and will purge away all sin." "Almsgiving will deliver from hell and make one perfectly righteous." We recognize this as heretical teaching, for giving alms cannot cleanse a man from sin. But such was the Jewish concept of almsgiving that they said, "Giving of alms will make restitution to God for sins that the giver has committed."

Now, the Pharisees had concluded that if a man gave, but gave in secret, he lost all benefit from giving. There must be an audience before one could gain any benefit from God through the giving. Thus they concluded they lost gains if there were no spectators.

So perverted was the law of love that the Lord had to correct their misinterpretation and their erroneous practice. So He said, "Take heed that ye do not your alms before men, to be seen of them; otherwise ye have no reward of your Father which is in heaven." Deuteronomy 15 had made it very clear that when they gave out of a heart of love in obedience to the Word of God, God would give blessing. But our Lord said the way to lose your blessing was to give for personal benefit. When one gives to be respected and admired by men, and when one gives to impress men with his beneficence, all basis for blessing from God is lost. He warned them of the Pharisees' misapplication of the truth of the Word of God. He said, "When thou doest thine alms, do not sound a trumpet before thee, as the hypocrites in the synagogues and the streets, that they may have glory of men. Verily, I say unto you, they have their reward."

To "blow your own horn" is to glory in what you have done, to attract attention to yourself. Our Lord said if you give and then attract attention to yourself, you have received your reward. You have received glory from men. But righteousness was designed to have its reward from God, and *does* have its reward from God whether it receives any reward from men at all. The Pharisees had substituted reward from men for the prospect of reward from God. How God looked at their deeds was insignificant to them because God's reward could not be immediately seen. They looked for some immediate, tangible result of their giving; so, to make certain when they gave to the poor that it attracted widespread attention, they gave in the midst of trumpet sounds so all men might see their generosity.

How often men give—not as an evidence of love toward

God, not as an evidence of obedience to the Word of God, not as a manifestation of righteousness that comes from God—but for the publicity they will gain. To what extent would our charities be supported if the recipients did not publish an annual list of donors? We give for publicity, and we have received our reward. We want publicity; we get it. But God does not count it an evidence of righteousness, nor a manifestation of love. The only love associated with blowing the trumpet is love for oneself. When men give as the Pharisees gave, to have glory of men, they are treating men as their justifiers. When they give to be admired of men, they operate on the basic assumption that their sin is against man; so, if they give to man, they can erase their sin against man. They, therefore, put themselves under the judgment of men and by their gifts seek to be excused by man from their sin. They fail to realize that sin, while it involves other men, is sin against the holy character of God. It is not men who need to be placated, but a holy, righteous God.

While the esteem of men can be purchased by material gifts, favor from God cannot be purchased. The Pharisees thought they could remove the injury done by sin by giving to men, by winning commendation from men, and they sought to ease the guilt of their conscience. The Lord said when they gave they were not to sound a trumpet to receive the honor and the glory, but rather, "When thou doest alms, let not thy left hand know what thy right hand doeth" (v. 3). What is done is to be done in secret. Righteousness is not a matter primarily between man and man. Righteousness is a matter between an individual and God. When you do not let your right hand know what your left hand is doing, you are conducting your affairs between yourself and God, unknown to anyone else. The individual who so manifests his righteousness, recognizes that he is responsible to God; that God is the source of blessing, the One he seeks to please and from whom he seeks approval.

Men have their own ways to promote themselves, and God becomes one of the most useful instruments in promoting ourself. Many politicians, just before election time, suddenly become active members of a church. They use God for their own ends. This is also a temptation to businessmen. Some feel they can further their business interests by affiliating with the right church. They expect to reap material benefits by association with that group or organization. They are using God. And how many times God is used at tax time as an income tax deduction? Don't try to use God to benefit yourself, to promote yourself, to attract glory to yourself.

If a man gives to receive glory for himself and to impress others with his generosity, he is not manifesting the righteousness of God which giving was designed to express. When a man gives out of love and obedience to the Word of God, when he gives to meet needs, he gives out of righteousness. To him the Lord said, "Thy Father which seeth in secret himself shall reward thee openly" (Mt 6:4).

The psalmist referred to this truth in Psalm 41:1: "Blessed is he that considereth the poor: the LORD will deliver him in time of trouble." The psalmist anticipated immediate blessing as a result of a righteous man's action, and was sure that God's reward would be evident in his time of need. But beyond the immediate reward, we may anticipate our Lord's approval when we stand before Him and hear His word, "Well done."

17

The Practice of Prayer

Matthew 6:6-15

When men assume responsibilities they do not know
how to discharge, they look for help. It is most natural to go
for help to the world around them. Often the standards that
the world or their friends set are far from the standards of
the Word of God. The disciples saw the Lord in prayer and
recognized that they as children of God had a responsibility to pray. But they did not know how to fulfill that
responsibility. So they might have looked around them to
learn how to pray. Instead of looking to the Lord as an
example of a life lived in fellowship with God, they might
have looked at the religious world to learn how to pray.
They might have turned their attention to the Pharisees,
who were great at praying. They might even have turned to
devotees of heathen gods to learn something from them
about how to pray.

In instructing the disciples in a life of godliness, the
Lord had to turn their attention away from the Pharisees,
who set religious standards for the Jews and from the
heathen priests after whom many patterned their experience, to Himself. The Pharisees were masters at using God.
They had found how to use Him to promote themselves.
The Pharisees were selfish and delighted to attract attention to themselves. Thus, when they gave alms or showed
charity, they sounded trumpets so that all men might be
attracted to them. They were not interested in giving to
meet the need of man, but they used giving as an opportun-

ity to display their own piety so they might be appreciated by men.

The Pharisees, from their knowledge of the Old Testament, recognized a responsibility to pray. Yet they did not examine the Scriptures to see how a man ought to pray, and why a man ought to pray. They perverted the forms and practice of prayer so that praying became another means to promote themselves before men. So the Lord said, "When thou prayest, thou shalt not be as the hypocrites are: for they love to pray standing in the synagogues and in the corners of the streets, that they may be seen of men. Verily I say unto you, They have their reward" (Mt 6: 5). In condemning the false practices of the Pharisees, He called the Pharisees "hypocrites."

The word *hypocrite*, in the original language, came from the theatrical world. It meant "to speak from under a mask." Men who played parts would put on a mask so those who saw the mask might know the character the actor was playing. An actor would play a number of parts in a play, and he would equip himself with a number of different masks. When he spoke the part of one, he would hold that mask before his face; when he spoke another part, he would change masks so he would be speaking behind the mask. One could not see the actor himself; he only saw the mask. The audience did not know the man; they knew only the part he played. Hypocrites, then, were men who were speaking "from under a mask."

The hypocritical Pharisees were corrupt, and their hearts a fountain of wickedness; but they held the mask of piety before their faces so men would be deceived and believe that they were something they were not. This was uniquely true when they prayed, for they did not pray to honor God. They did not pray to humble themselves. They prayed to build themselves up in men's esteem. And they did not look to God when they prayed. Prayer to them was pointless unless there was a large audience they could impress with their piety, their oratory, and the length of their prayers. There they stood, resplendent in their robes, with their eyes not turned heavenward to honor God or down to earth to signify their unworthiness. Many stood with their eyes upon the crowd and, when they gained the approval of the crowd, they considered themselves successful in prayer.

To those who might pattern their relationship to God on the hypocrisy of the Pharisees, the Lord said, "When thou prayest, thou shalt not be as the hypocrites are: for they love to pray standing in the synagogues and in the corners of the streets [i.e., where men gather], that they may be seen of men." The Pharisees were using religion. They were using God for selfish ends so they might be built up in the esteem of people. Since this was their motive in praying, they had their desire satisfied. They wanted the esteem of men, the approbation of the crowd, and by their oratory they received the approval of men. They received what they went after. They had their reward. They had no reward from God, for He did not approve such hypocrisy. They had no reward in their hearts or satisfaction from having enjoyed a relationship to God. Their only reward was the congratulations at the close of their prayer. How easy it is to seemingly fill our responsibility to God to gain the approval of men and not to pattern our actions according to the Word and will of God.

While man's faith in God will manifest itself in a man's relationship to men, a man's faith in God is a matter between himself and God alone. When one's religion is used to impress men, God disavows it as providing any basis for His approval. Multitudes assemble themselves in churches, not out of a heart of love and devotion to God, nor because they recognize a sense of obligation to come together with God's people around His Word to fellowship with their Father. They gather together to maintain an image, a reputation before men. They go through empty forms of worship, devoid of any reality. They are there to impress men, and the Lord said they will get what they want. They will have their reward, but not from God.

Pharisees as a whole had no concept of praying in private. It was utterly foreign to them. They considered it a waste of time because, if you went into your room behind a closed door and prayed, whom could you impress? So our Lord instructed the disciples on the pattern of godliness in the matter of praying. After mentioning the public praying of the Pharisees, He said, "When thou prayest, enter into thy closet [your secret place, into your room], and when thou hast shut thy door [so no eye can see what you are doing when you are alone with God], pray to thy Father which is in secret; and thy Father which seeth in secret shall reward thee openly" (v. 6).

The Lord tried to impress His hearers with the truth that prayer is essentially a private communication between a child and his Father. Two who are in love require privacy to properly communicate. Little real communication is possible in public. Volumes can be communicated in moments when there is privacy. In the busyness of life, communication with the Father is impossible unless there is privacy. That is why the Lord said if we are to communicate with the Father we must go to our room and shut the door. One prying eye can spoil communication. As soon as we are conscious of one observer, the privacy necessary to intimate communication is gone, and we become conscious of the observer rather than the Father with whom we are talking. Therefore the Pharisees could not communicate with the Father when they gathered an audience to hear their prayers. Prayer is private communication.

Does this mean, then, there is no place for public prayer? No. For when two hearts, or even two hundred hearts, are united as one in praying, they are occupied with the Father and not with observers. Many can be one when hearts are united in subjection to God and join in worship. But if some do not unite, then prayer is disrupted. That is why serious attention must be given to public prayer, lest we talk to one another and not to God.

Not only did men have the pattern set by the Pharisees who believed in public praying, but also they had a pattern set by the devotees of heathen gods who thought the efficacy of prayer depended upon repetition. The heathen thought their gods were banqueting and had to be enticed away from the banquet table; or their gods were engaged in the pursuit of pleasure and had no time to listen to those who prayed to them; or their gods were sleeping and had to be awakened. So they thought they should say their prayers over and over again so that at some time, when their gods were not eating, drinking, playing, or sleeping they might hear. The heathen never knew when the gods would pay attention to their cry.

Some had concluded that God was preoccupied with His own things and had no time for His children; therefore, they had better pray repetitiously so that in an unguarded moment they might attract His attention. The Lord said, "When ye pray, use not vain [empty] repetitions, as the heathen do: for they think that they shall be heard for their much speaking" (v. 7).

The fallacy of the heathen concept of God is so evident that He said, "Be not ye therefore like unto them: for your Father knoweth what things ye have need of, before ye ask" (v. 8). A faithful father anticipates the needs of his children. An experienced father does not need to be informed what his child needs because he has anticipated the need. Prayer is not designed to inform God what our needs are; as a faithful Father He knows. Prayer is designed to let God know that we know our need, and in our need we trust Him to provide. Since God already knows and is willing to meet the need of His children, it is not necessary to inform Him by endless repetition. Prayer need not be public, because communication is private. Prayer need not be repetitious, because God already knows.

Then, after Jesus criticized the false practices of the Pharisees, He moved on (vv. 9-13) to give us a model of prayer, although not one to be prayed repetitiously. Our Lord showed the disciples the areas in life with which prayer ought to be concerned. Our Lord's words defined five areas our Father is concerned about, with which we ought to be concerned.

First, the believer is concerned with God's person. When you pray, say, "Our Father which art in heaven, Hallowed [holy, honored, respected] be thy name" (v. 9). God is our Father. He is the sovereign Creator ("which art in heaven"). He is exalted over all. He is a Father whose name is above all, and over all, before whom His children bow in reverence, respect, love, and trust ("hallowed be thy name"). We are occupied first of all with a Person.

Second, we ought to be concerned about God's *program*. "Thy kingdom come. Thy will be done in earth, as it is in heaven." Throughout the Old Testament God had promised the coming of the Lord Jesus Christ. As a Saviour and a King He would establish a Kingdom on earth over which He would rule. God's program centered in a Person He purposed to enthrone so that He might rule as King of kings, and Lord of lords. Such was the hope of Israel. The true child of God concerns himself not so much about his own plans and desires as he does with the determinate program of God to enthrone Jesus Christ. All history until the end of time presses toward the enthronement of Jesus Christ, who will sit on David's throne. The Christian concerns himself not with his own circumstances and needs but with what occupies the heart of God, the exaltation of His Son.

Third, the child of God is concerned about God's *provision* for his own needs. "Give us this day our daily bread." The child trusts his Father day by day. To keep us trusting, God does not provide us with a pantry and a freezer so that we come once or twice a year to refill the larder. "Give us today's bread today." Your needs from day to day may vary. You may have physical needs, mental needs, emotional or spiritual needs. God's grace provides as we trust, but He provides one day at a time. So the child of God, in his communication with God, is concerned about today's needs.

Fourth, the child of God is concerned about *personal purity*, "Forgive us our debts, as we forgive our debtors." Since God has provided for forgiveness for His sinning child, that child avails himself of forgiveness for daily sins. If we forgive those who sin against us, how much more will God forgive His children who seek His forgiveness? God's child is concerned about personal holiness.

Fifth, the Christian is concerned with God's *protection*.

"Lead us not into temptation, but deliver us from evil." The Old Testament promised God would give His angels charge over us to bear us up in their hands lest we dash our foot against a stone. God's eye is on us and He protects so that we might walk through this world as becomes our sonship with Jesus Christ. We trust Him to keep us from falling into sin when beset by temptation, and to deliver us when attacked by the evil one.

These are matters with which the child of God should be occupied. An individual in whose life prayer does not play an important part is one out of harmony with the heart of God. For as a Father, He desires the love of His children; if love is not communicated, the heart of the lover is not satisfied. Prayer is a communication between a child and his Father concerning God's person, God's program, God's provision, God's protection, and our purity. May God make us a people who learn to pray.

18

Why Fast?

Matthew 6:16-24

One of the major medical problems facing the people of the United States is overweight. While multitudes destroy their bodies by dope, alcohol, and tobacco, a far greater multitude are destroying themselves by being overweight. In the light of that, the Lord's words are most pertinent:

> Moreover when ye fast, be not, as the hypocrites, of a sad countenance: for they disfigure their faces, that they may appear unto men to fast. Verily I say unto you, They have their reward. But thou, when thou fastest, annoint thine head, and wash thy face; that thou appear not unto men to fast, but unto thy Father which is in secret: and thy Father, which seeth in secret, shall reward thee openly (Mt 6:16-18).

Any thought of fasting when we have the wherewithal to provide bountiful repasts is utterly repugnant. What place does fasting have in the life of the child of God? Food is one of God's blessings provided by His goodness for the enjoyment of His creation. Food serves a number of different purposes. The first and obvious one is that food was given by God to sustain the body. At the time of creation God said, "And to every beast of the earth, and to every fowl of the air, and to every thing that creepeth upon the earth, wherein there is life, I have given every green herb for meat [food]: and it was so" (Gen 1:30). From the time of creation God provided food for His creatures to sustain the body.

Genesis 2:9 reads, "Out of the ground made the LORD

141

God to grow every tree that is pleasant to the sight, and good for food." Then after the devastating judgment of the flood, "Every moving thing that liveth shall be meat [food] for you; even as the green herb have I given you all things" (Gen 9:3). So vegetables and meat were provided by God to sustain the physical body.

In the second place, food provides man with fellowship. One of the principal concepts of fellowship in the New Testament is associated with eating. In Acts 2:42, following the great sermon by Peter that brought thousands to a saving knowledge of Christ, we read, "They continued steadfastly in the apostles' doctrine and fellowship, and in breaking of bread [in eating] and in prayer." For one believer to eat with another provided a basis for fellowship.

This is brought out again in 1 Corinthians 11, where the apostle has to correct the misuse of the Lord's table. He said, "Wherefore, my brethren, when ye come together to eat, tarry one for another. And if any man hunger, let him eat at home; that ye come not together unto condemnation [judgment]" (v. 33-34). There we discover it was the practice of the church to have a meal together. Then at the conclusion of their fellowship together around the meal, they would pass the bread and the cup so they who had enjoyed fellowship with one another might have fellowship with God.

In Revelation the Lord said, "Behold, I stand at the door, and knock: if any man hear my voice, and open the door, I will come in to him, and will sup with him, and he with me" (3:20). When the Lord described fellowship, He described it as sitting down to a meal. Again in John 21:9, when the Lord wanted to enjoy fellowship with the apostles after His resurrection, He built a fire, broiled fish, and provided bread, and then said "Come, and dine" (v. 12).

Since man needs not only to sustain his body but also his soul, God gave him food to eat. As he partook of food, his body was sustained; as he ate with others, his soul was sustained through their fellowship together. There is nothing more lonely than to have to eat alone. When we merely sustain the body with food, the food has not fulfilled its entire purpose; it was designed by God to provide a basis for fellowship between individuals.

In the third place there is a Godward aspect to eating. Not only does it contribute something to the body and to the soul, but also it satisfies man in his relationship to God. In Matthew 6:11, when our Lord gave instruction concerning prayer, He said we should pray, "Give us this day our daily bread." When we pray for daily bread we register our dependence upon God for what will sustain body and soul. When a man depends on God, he honors Him. In 1 Timothy, Paul said, there will be some who will propagate doctrines of demons, "Forbidding to marry, and commanding to abstain from meats which God hath created to be received with thanksgiving of them that believe and know the truth. For every creature of God is good [for food], and nothing to be refused, if it be received with thanksgiving" (4:3-4). When an individual sits down to a meal, gives God thanks for that meal, and eats the meal with thanksgiving, he honors God. So eating food has its Godward aspect; food is to be eaten with thanksgiving. God designed this body to be sustained by food. He became the One who provided for the needs of His creation. In providing food He provided a basis of fellowship among the creatures, through which the creature could express his praise, his thanksgiving, and his dependence upon God. Food is good and is one of God's blessings; but like all of God's blessings and provisions it may be misused.

The Pharisees, who were adept at using God for their own selfish ends, used this blessing from God as they did His other blessings, and perverted food for their own selfish end. It was necessary for the Lord to correct the Pharisees' attitude toward food so they might pattern their conduct according to the righteous standard of God.

Fasting had an important place throughout the Old Testament. The root of the word translated *to fast* means "to afflict the soul" or "to deny oneself." One who fasted did not question that food was good and designed by God to provide for both the body and soul, to provide manward and Godward fellowship. But he expressed many things by voluntarily abstaining from food for a season.

Men fasted for many reasons in Old Testament times. First of all, men fasted for religious reasons. Leviticus 23:26-29 gives the rule concerning the Day of Atonement, the central day in Israel's religious calendar.

> The LORD spake unto Moses, saying, Also on the tenth day of this seventh month there shall be a day of atonement: it shall be an holy convocation unto you; and ye shall afflict your souls [the word *afflict* is related to fasting], and offer an offering made by fire unto the LORD. And ye shall do no work in that same day: for it is a day of atonement, to make an atonement for you before the LORD your God. For whatsoever soul it be that shall not be afflicted [will not fast] in that same day, he shall be cut off from among his people.

The Day of Atonement was a fast day, and the people were to abstain from food during the day so that they might give their entire attention to the day's focal point, the slaying of the goat and application of its blood to the mercy seat as a covering for the nation's sins.

Then we find that fasting was associated with a manifestation of sorrow. The experience of David is recorded in 2 Samuel. Abner, David's captain, had been slain, and David was overcome with grief. "When all the people came to cause David to eat meat while it was yet day, David sware, saying, So do God to me, or more also, if I taste bread, or ought else, till the sun be down" (3:35). David expressed grief at the loss of his beloved friend and trusted captain by refusing a morsel of food from sunup to sundown. He demonstrated his sorrow to the nation by fasting.

Some fasted because of a burden they bore. We have the tender note concerning Hannah who expressed distress at her childlessness by fasting: "Therefore she wept, and did not eat" (1 Sa 1:7). Hannah was grieved, and her fasting was a sign of distress of heart.

Disappointment was expressed by a fast in 1 Kings 21. Ahab coveted Naboth's vineyard, and Naboth would not sell the vineyard to him. As a result, "Ahab came into his house heavy and displeased because of the word that Naboth the Jezreelite had spoken unto him: for he had said, I will not give thee the inheritance of my fathers. And he laid him down upon his bed, and turned away his face, and would eat no bread" (v. 4). Ahab fasted because of his disappointment.

Sometimes sympathy for another was expressed by a fast in the Old Testament. David said, "As for me, when they were sick, my clothing was sackcloth: I humbled my soul with fasting" (Ps 35:13). His fasting was a sign of sympathy for one who was ill.

Daniel 10 records the experience of God's prophet who, at the end of seventy years of Babylonian captivity uttered a great prayer of confession in acknowledgment of guilt. "In those days I Daniel was mourning three full weeks. I ate no pleasant bread, neither came flesh nor wine in my mouth, neither did I annoint myself at all, till three whole weeks were fulfilled" (vv. 2-3). For three weeks, Daniel fasted because his heart was burdened by the sin of his people, and he gave himself to prayer of confession. His fasting was associated with confession of sin.

In Ezra prayer and fasting are again joined together. Ezra said, "I proclaimed a fast there, at the river of Ahava, that we might afflict ourselves before our God, to seek of him a right way for us, and for our little ones, and for our substance" (8:21). His fast signified his dependence on God and his desire to know God's will.

Again in Esther the same truth is presented. Esther, contrary to the national law, was to enter the presence of the king so that she might present a petition. "Esther bade them return Mordecai this answer, Go, gather together all the Jews that are present in Shushan, and fast ye for me, and neither eat nor drink three days, night or day: I also and my maidens will fast likewise; and so will I go in unto the king, which is not according to the law, and if I perish, I perish" (Est 4:15-16). For three days before Esther approached the king the people fasted and prayed she would be preserved and that the king would grant her request.

We find from this association between prayer and fasting that according to the Jewish concept fasting was a way to give weight to prayer. They expected God to hear their prayer, but when they fasted with their praying they considered that more weight was given to the prayer. So when one was under a tremendous burden, to supplement and implement his prayers and give his prayers power before God, he abstained from food. Sometimes, as we found in these verses, fasting was from sunrise to sunset. Sometimes the fasting was referred to as a three-day period, or even for a three-week period. Sometimes a fast involved total abstinence from food; other times it involved abstinence from what Daniel called pleasant, or good, or rich food, which intimated existence on the barest kind of subsistence.

But in each case, what fasting meant was that the individual was renouncing the natural demands of his body and the natural joys of eating, and registering a total dependence upon God. He was trusting God to sustain him day by day as he ate food. When he abstained from food, he was trusting God to sustain him in a supernatural way. It was expected God would sustain the body that had eaten food. So, when one went without food, he was expecting God to sustain him in a supernatural way. The fast, then, registered a total dependence upon God in a time of sorrow, distress, sympathy, confession of sin, or in a time of prayer.

In the story of the Pharisee who went down to pray, the Pharisee said: "I fast twice in the week" (Lk 18:12). It had become the custom of the Jews to fast every Monday and Thursday, from sunrise to sunset. They went without food until the sun set, and then they would break the fast. But they did not fast because of sorrow for sin, nor to give themselves to prayer, nor because of some bereavement or distress or disappointment, or out of sympathy for someone who was being tested. They fasted to be seen of men, to build themselves a reputation for being dependent upon God. They claimed they were dependent upon God, but there was no dependence in mind or heart. God said that was hypocrisy, and He detested it.

Lest a man miss the fact that the Pharisees were fasting, they would cover their faces with ashes, the Old Testament sign of mourning. When a Jew laid aside his robe and put on sackcloth and put ashes on his face, he appeared to men to have a heart tender before God or to be responding to the needs of someone with whom he was fellowshipping. So the Jews would cover their faces with ashes and stand in a public place by the hour, so men would honor them for their devotion to God. In the face of this practice the Lord said, "When ye fast, be not, as the hypocrites, of a sad countenance: for they disfigure their faces, that they may appear unto men to fast. Verily I say unto you, They have their reward" (Mt 6:16).

Men looked on the outward appearance and counted these men to be pious because they went through these outward forms. But it was the only reward they had, for God is not satisfied with the proud heart that finds delight in the applause of men. "When thou fastest, annoint thine head, and wash thy face" (v. 17). Oil, in the Old Testament, was a sign of rejoicing. Olive oil was rubbed over the face to give it a bright, shining appearance, to show the joy of the Lord. Our Lord said, "When you fast, let it show the joy of the Lord."

The danger we face as we receive food God has provided to sustain the body and provide fellowship with men is that we will take care of the body by eating, and take care of the soul by fellowship, and will ignore God. How true this often is. God desires us to be occupied with Him, not with the flesh. What we draw from fellowship with Him is greater than what we draw from fellowship with men. "And thy Father, which seeth in secret, shall reward thee openly."

19

Treasure in Earth or Heaven?

Matthew 6:19-29

With a sweep of His hands, the Lord Jesus Christ brushed aside the righteousness of the Pharisees. He said, "Except your righteousness shall exceed the righteousness of the scribes and Pharisees, ye shall in no case enter into the Kingdom of Heaven" (Mt 5:20). In chapter 6, the Lord showed that not only their *interpretation* of the Law but also their *practice* of the Law was erroneous.

In Matthew 6, the Lord showed that the Pharisees' idea of wealth was not true. He said, "Lay not up for yourselves treasures upon earth, where moth and rust doth corrupt, and where thieves break through and steal: but lay up for yourselves treasures in heaven, where neither moth nor rust doth corrupt, and where thieves do not break through nor steal: For where your treasure is, there will your heart be also" (vv. 19-21). The Pharisees were characterized not only by hypocrisy, but also by avarice, or covetousness. The two go hand in hand. One of the earliest examples of this in the Scriptures is recorded in 1 Samuel 2. The two sons of the high priest, Eli, were men of responsibility in the religious life of Israel. But they were hypocrites, and this manifested itself in greed. The Law had provided that a priest was to be supplied food from the offerings brought to the Lord. But the offering was the Lord's offering and belonged to Him. The priest was permitted to have the breast and the right thigh, according to Leviticus 7:30-35. But Hophni and Phineas, the sons of Eli, demanded that, before the offering was offered to the Lord, they be permit-

148

ted to select a portion that pleased them; then the remainder was to be offered to the Lord. They were covetous. They were greedy. They were hypocritical. "The sin of the young men was very great before the Lord: for the men abhorred the offering of the Lord" (1 Sa 2:17). They presided at the sacrifice but had no respect for sacrifice and the God to whom it was offered.

The Pharisees had become a class of people characterized by hypocrisy and greed. Their attitude toward material things finds its roots in Deuteronomy 28. At the conclusion of the forty years' wilderness experience, God brought Israel again to the border of the promised land. God through Moses laid down the principle by which He would deal with the nation: "It shall come to pass, if thou shalt hearken diligently unto the voice of the LORD thy God, to observe and do all His commandments which I command thee this day, that the LORD thy God will set thee on high above all nations of the earth: and all these blessings shall come on thee, and overtake thee, if thou shalt hearken unto the voice of the LORD thy God" (Deu 28:1-2). Before He enumerated the blessings, God stated the principle that obedience to the revealed Word and conformity to the righteous standards of His holiness would bring blessing upon His people. We discover that these blessings are all material ones: "Blessed shalt thou be in the city, and blessed shalt thou be in the field. Blessed shall be the fruit of thy body, and the fruit of thy ground, and the fruit of thy cattle, the increase of thy kine, and the flocks of thy sheep. Blessed shalt be thy basket and thy store. Blessed shalt thou be when thou comest in, blessed shalt thou be when thou goest out" (Deu 28:3-6). Material blessings were promised when they came into the promised land, if they walked in obedience to the requirements of the Word of God.

God laid down the principle of discipline for disobedience, between verse 15 and the conclusion of Deuteronomy 28.

> It shall come to pass, if thou wilt not hearken unto the voice of the LORD thy God, to observe to do all his command-

ments and his statutes which I command thee this day; that all these curses shall come upon thee, and overtake thee. Cursed shalt thou be in the city, and cursed shalt thou be in the field. Cursed shall be thy basket and thy store. Cursed shall be the fruit of thy body, and the fruit of thy land, the increase of thy kine, and the flocks of thy sheep. Cursed shalt thou be when thou comest in, and cursed shalt thou be when thou goest out (vv. 15-19).

With many other words Moses admonished the people, laying before them the principle that righteousness would bring divine blessing, but disobedience would bring divine judgment.

On the basis of this principle the Pharisees built a system in which they sought to enrich themselves by doing things the Law demanded. The Pharisee, as our Lord said in Matthew 6, gave to the poor, prayed incessantly, and fasted twice a week. But he did it not because that was the righteousness of the Law; he did it to obtain material prosperity from God. He wanted to bind God to pour out blessing on him because of his righteousness. The Pharisees misapplied a scripture verse to convey their concept toward material possessions: "Whom the Lord loveth, He maketh rich." The acquisition of material wealth became the greatest goal in life for the Pharisees. It was a sure sign their righteousness satisfied God and that God had rewarded them by pouring material blessing upon them.

Solomon sought to deter the nation in their pursuit of this philosophy in Proverbs 23:4: "Labor not to be rich," that is, do not make it the goal of your life to obtain riches. Then Solomon explained why he had given this warning, "A faithful man shall abound with blessings: but he that maketh haste to be rich shall not be innocent" (28:20). Solomon recognized that a man whose goal is to accumulate material wealth will ultimately stoop to any means to attain that goal. He will defile himself in the sight of God to reach his own ends.

In spite of these warnings, Luke 16:14 records, "The Pharisees also, who were covetous, heard all these things:

and they derided him." Moses had given a commandment to safeguard the children of Israel against greed; he said in Exodus 20:17, "Thou shalt not covet." Whether the covetousness was of a neighbor's wife, a neighbor's land, a neighbor's house, or a neighbor's material wealth, the prohibition was there. But the Pharisees, despising the Law, had perverted His righteousness in their avariciousness. Because they were covetous, they rejected His message. To those who have a wrong concept of wealth, our Lord spoke concerning true wealth: "Lay not up for yourselves treasures upon earth."

The phrase "upon earth" is significant. This earth was created by God, and when He had finished His creation He looked at it and saw that it was good (Gen 2:31). God placed man upon this earth, and man rebelled against Him. Because of his rebellion, he came under divine judgment, which extended not only to the creature who had sinned but also to all creation. The earth was cursed when Adam sinned, which means the gold, silver, diamonds, rubies, and emeralds—earth's treasures—are under the curse.

Peter said that divine judgment one day will fall upon this earth and it will be destroyed by fire (2 Pe 3:7, 10, 12). Out of the ashes of this judged earth, according to Revelation 21, God will create new heavens and new earth wherein will dwell righteousness. The fact emphasized is that all earth is under a curse and subject to divine wrath and will one day be destroyed. When a man accumulates what is of the earth, he accumulates that which by its very nature is temporary, with no abiding worth.

Our Lord used three graphic figures in Matthew 6:19 to emphasize the temporary nature of material things. He spoke first of the moth, which destroys. Then he spoke of rust, which causes decay. Then he referred to the thief, who steals. What men give their lives to may be destroyed or decayed, and ultimately will depart forever.

Contrary to that, our Lord said, "Lay up for yourselves treasures in heaven, where neither moth nor rust doth corrupt, and where thieves do not break through nor steal"

(Mt 6:20). Although the earth is under divine judgment, no sin comes into the presence of God, and there is neither defilement nor destruction. No adversary can come to cause true riches to depart. So He invited men, as an evidence of true righteousness, to seek true wealth, to lay up permanent treasures in heaven.

The Lord Jesus recognized that a man's goals determine the course of his life, and the end to which men press determines the character of life. He said, "Where your treasure is, there will your heart be also" (Mt 6:21). What a man loves he pursues, and the preeminent love of a man's life determines the course of his life. If, in covetousness and greed, we pursue what is earthly, corrupt, and transitory, our conduct in life will never manifest a righteousness pleasing to God. Only when we have a new goal and attitude toward material things will our life conform to the standards of holiness given in the Word of God.

Our Lord did not condemn wealth, but He warned against loving wealth. Our Lord was not concerned with what a man has, but with a man's attitude toward what he has. The Scripture does not condemn the accumulation of wealth but, when God gives a man wealth, He holds him responsible as a steward. Our Lord did not say we should give away everything we have and put ourselves on welfare. What He said was, "Guard your affections."

We might ask ourselves, "What is treasure in heaven?" The Word of God makes it very clear what Christ had in mind. Paul stated in 1 Timothy 6:6 what constitutes true wealth. "Godliness with contentment is great gain." We may paraphrase this, "Godliness with contentment is a man's greatest treasure" or "Godliness is heavenly wealth." Paul also showed that material wealth is temporary: "We brought nothing into this world, and it is certain we can carry nothing out. And having food and raiment let us be therewith content" (vv. 7-8). The well-known phrase, *you can't take it with you,* has a biblical foundation—we brought nothing in, and we take nothing out when we leave. Paul emphasized that material things are related to this life and have no relationship to the life to come.

How little of this principle the Pharaohs of Egypt knew! In the Cairo Museum, you might see the treasures of almost incomputable worth taken from the tombs of the kings. This vast wealth was buried with the Pharaohs, for they hoped to carry along with them to a future life what they had so richly enjoyed on earth. But the Pharaohs are gone, and they left their riches behind. Our museums are enriched because they sought to take their wealth along but could not. The biblical principle is, "We brought nothing into this world, and it is certain we can carry nothing out."

Paul spoke of the dangers facing the wealthy. "They that will be rich fall into temptation and a snare" (1 Ti 6:9). He did not say "those who are rich," but those who *desire* to be rich are the ones who fall into temptation and into many foolish lusts which will drown them in destruction. "The love of money is the root of all evil" (1 Ti 6:10). Paul did not say that money is the root of all evil, but that *love* of it is. A man can *have* wealth, can surround himself by material things, but still not make wealth the goal of his life. But he cannot *love* those things without making them a controlling factor in his life. Therefore, Paul warned against a desire to be rich and a love of what has already been accumulated, "which while some coveted after, they have erred from the faith, and pierced themselves through with many sorrows" (v. 10).

Then Paul came to the conclusion of what he wanted to teach about godliness being a man's wealth, and defined for us what is heavenly treasure: "But thou, O man of God, flee these things [covetousness, lust, avarice, greed, love of material things]; and follow after righteousness, godliness, faith, love, patience, meekness" (v. 11). These are things God counts heavenly treasures, the things a man does not leave behind when he comes into the presence of the Father. They are the things he sends on ahead to prepare a gracious entrance into the Lord's presence. These virtues are called, in Galatians 5, "the fruit of the Spirit," and it is that fruit Paul called a man's "great gain." Our Lord called

it treasure in heaven and He warned against loving what is
earthly and ignoring what is heavenly.

We can be deceived by our own affections. We can love
money and at the same time disavow any interest in it. We
can lust after the material while claiming to be spiritually
minded. Only the Spirit of God, who searches the heart, is
capable of revealing our motives, our goals, and our love so
they are brought into line with the teaching of the Word of
God. "Lay not up for yourselves treasures on earth."
Earthly treasure is not true wealth; true wealth is godliness.

20

God or Mammon?

Matthew 6:22-24

A baby is born into the world with a clenched fist, as though he were prepared to hold onto what is his. When a man accumulates material wealth, he feels like a king acquiring subjects over whom he can rule. When he spends the money, he feels like a general sending armies into combat to do his will. Avarice is characteristic of the natural man. He loves to accumulate, and he loves what he accumulates. He finds contentment in what he can grasp, and see, and hold to his breast. The Lord, in the Sermon on the Mount, warned his hearers against the love of material things.

In Matthew 6:22-24, the Lord continued teaching the danger of loving material things:

> The light of the body is the eye: if therefore thine eye be single, thy whole body shall be full of light. But if thine eye be evil, thy whole body shall be full of darkness. If therefore the light that is in thee be darkness, how great is that darkness! No man can serve two masters: for either he will hate the one, and love the other; or else he will hold to the one, and despise the other. Ye cannot serve God and mammon.

The Jews used the eye figuratively in a moral sense; to have an "evil eye" signified having a distorted view of things. An individual who can focus both eyes clearly on a given object sees the object without distortion; but the individual who lacks the capacity to focus both eyes has distorted vision. The physical problem of distorted vision taught the Jews a deep spiritual truth: a man may have a perverted view of things and not understand their true nature, their true values, or their true worth. So to have a clear, undistorted—or, as our translation says, "single"—vision, signified a proper perspective. The opposite of this was double vision, or a distorted viewpoint.

This Jewish concept came from several passages in the Old Testament. In the laws governing social conduct laid down for the children of Israel, Moses said,

> If there be among you a poor man of one of thy brethren within any of thy gates in thy land which the LORD thy God giveth thee, thou shalt not harden thine heart, nor shut thine hand from thy poor brother: but thou shalt open thine hand wide unto him, and shalt surely lend him sufficient for his need, in that which he wanteth. Beware that there be not a thought in thy wicked heart, saying, The seventh year, the year of release, is at hand; and thine eye be evil against thy poor brother, and thou givest him nought; and he cry unto the LORD against thee, and it be sin unto thee (Deu 15:7-9).

Moses taught the children of Israel that they had a responsibility toward a brother in need. If a brother's need came to a man's attention and he shut up his heart and refused to give to him what he needed, he had a wicked heart. That individual was blinded, and his vision distorted by his greed. He might recognize the need but love his possessions to the extent that he refused to contribute toward the need of his brother. Moses said this was evidence of a wicked heart. The evil eye likewise revealed a distorted view of things and reflected a moral perversion.

The same truth is presented in Proverbs 23:6-7: "Eat thou not the bread of him that hath an evil eye, neither desire thou his dainty meats: for as he thinketh in his heart, so is he: Eat and drink, saith he to thee; but his heart is not with thee." Here Solomon spoke of a wealthy man able to provide a banquet table. If he has an evil eye, he will resent the food you eat and his heart will be controlled by bitterness. He may have an abundance, but he resents what you eat. So Solomon said, "Eat not the bread of him that hath an evil eye." The evil eye spoke of a distorted view of the value of things.

The same truth is found again in Proverbs 28:22: "He that hasteth to be rich hath an evil eye, and considereth not that poverty shall come upon him." Once again, the man who bends every effort to accumulate material possessions has an evil eye, a distorted view of the value and permanence of wealth. He thinks he will retain his wealth forever and does not realize, as Paul says, that we brought nothing into this world, and can take nothing from it. He takes what is temporary and attributes to it eternal worth. That perverted view, Solomon said, reveals an "evil eye."

From these Old Testament Scriptures we see that while the Lord's words are strange to our ears because we do not use the same idiom, they conveyed a concept well-established in the minds of his listeners. Our Lord said, "the light of the body is the eye." It is the eye that brings light so man can see. It is self-evident that where there is no light there can be no sight. Our Lord taught the moral and ethical lesson that, unless there is light from God, there can be no proper interpretation of what is of true worth. Until the light of God shines upon something, we do not know its true character.

Now, because these Jews had a distorted view of the value of material possessions, our Lord had to say, "If thine eye be evil [as it is, if you have a distorted view of the value of material possessions], thy whole body shall be full of darkness" (6:23). What the Jews deemed to be a blessing from God our Lord said was evidence of a perverted outlook of darkness within.

The rabbis had taught that the way to keep the soul healthy was to give generously. To be miserly was to distort the vision. If one was miserly, the eye of the soul would be blinded. But what the rabbis had taught was ignored by the Pharisees, and our Lord said that they were in blindness or darkness.

If a man does not have a right view of material things, eventually he will have a distorted view of life as a whole. If he has double vision concerning material things, he will adopt an entirely false set of goals for life. Sooner or later he will submit himself to those material things, and they will have made him a slave. Greed for things or money is a most unrelenting master. The claims of loved ones; the needs of relatives or friends; the demands of country, honor, comfort, and even of health itself may be overlooked; a man will abandon all when the acquisition of money becomes the obsession of his life. Avarice is the most unrelenting master in the world. The Lord emphasized this when He said that no man can be faithful to two masters at the same time. "Either he will hate the one, and love the other; or else he will hold to the one, and despise the other. Ye cannot serve God and mammon" (v. 24).

"Mammon" is a personalization of God's chief rival —money or material things. Our Lord viewed the acquisition of wealth as a goal that brings a man into the most abject slavery, that prevents him from discharging his responsibility as one enslaved to Jesus Christ. He becomes enslaved instead to money and can serve no one else, least of all God. When a man is consumed by a passion to accumulate material things, there is room for no other love. The Lord did not condemn *possession* of wealth. He did condemn *being possessed by* that wealth. He viewed the love of money as gross idolatry.

Paul wrote, "Mortify therefore your members which are upon the earth; fornication, uncleanness, inordinate affection, evil concupiscence, and covetousness, which is idolatry" (Col 3:5). Covetousness is idolatry. Israel in the Old Testament despised the God who had the right, because He had redeemed them from Egypt, to rule over them, and they submitted themselves to the idolatrous gods of the nations among whom they dwelt. Likewise, Paul said that, when a man loves money, he repudiates the right of the God who redeemed him to rule over him, and he submits himself to another god. Just as Israel fell into all sorts of abominable practices because they followed false gods, so, Paul said, the man who makes the love of money the love of his life will find himself stooping to abominable practices.

Wealth is viewed in Scripture as a trust. It is never viewed as an end, but as a means to an end. It is viewed as God's blessing, but every blessing entails a responsibility. What God entrusts to a man is not to be used for selfish enjoyment but for the benefit and blessing of others. A man cannot be righteous and avaricious at the same time. A man cannot be godly and greedy at the same time. A man cannot be a lover of God and a lover of material things at the same time. Man cannot be a faithful servant of Jesus Christ and sell himself as a bond servant to money at the same time.

Our Lord was dealing not only with actions but also with basic attitudes toward life. In effect, He was asking a question, "What to you is the highest good in life?" In our society, multitudes would have to confess they measure goodness by accumulated material possessions. A man is said to have it made when he is in a high tax bracket. Such is a revelation of the distorted vision that our Lord said plunges the whole soul into moral darkness. This passage calls upon us to take a hard look at the things by which we set such store and ask ourselves, "If those things were suddenly taken away, how rich would I be?" Hear the Word of the Lord again: "No man can serve two masters: for either he will hate the one, and love the other; or else he will hold to one, and despise the other." You cannot serve God and God's chief rival, material things. What really matters in life? Gold or godliness?

21

The Unreasonableness of Worry

Matthew 6:25-34

It is easy for a man to make a god out of material things, but when he gives his devotion to that god, he finds himself enslaved to the most tyrannical master. That preoccupation with material things the Lord dealt with in this portion of the Sermon on the Mount. A mark of a righteous man is his preoccupation with God. When a man sets aside the God of righteousness and accepts the god of material things, he soon conforms to materialistic standards. He becomes greedy, covetous, and totally preoccupied with material possessions. If a man becomes preoccupied with material things and they become the goal of his life, he soon becomes anxious about his physical needs. He becomes preoccupied with what he will eat, what he will drink, what clothing he will wear, where he will live. This anxious care comes because of a lack of trust in God. When a man ceases to trust God for his needs, he eventually becomes enslaved to material things. Our Lord taught those who were concerned with righteousness that one cannot serve God and material things at the same time.

A man who serves God trusts God; and he trusts God not only for eternity but also for time. He trusts God for his soul and for his body as well. A man may give himself to many things. He may give himself to the gratification of physical desire, but as he grows old what he served as a god may relax its grip upon him and he can be delivered from its dominion. A man may give himself to the pursuit of pleasure, but the older he gets, the less they may entice him. He finds he can slip out from under the grasp of the god of pleasure he has served. But if a man gives himself to material things as his god, he finds the older he gets, the tighter the grip of that god upon him. He becomes more rather than less enslaved. Therefore our Lord said (Mt 6:25), "Therefore I say unto you, Take no thought [do not have anxious care or give no place to anxiety concerning] for your life [that is your physical or material life], what ye shall eat, or what ye shall drink; nor yet for your body, what ye shall put on."

The Lord recognized that a man in his covetousness may devote his life entirely to providing food, shelter, and clothing, and it becomes the circumference of his life. In the light of the fact a man cannot serve God and material things at the same time, our Lord commands, "Do not become preoccupied with these material things." Let not anxiety or anxious care have a place in your heart concerning these material things.

Paul has a reassuring word, "My God shall supply all your need (Phil 4:19). The body cannot exist long without food or drink. It needs shelter and clothing, and these things preoccupy an unrighteous man. God will provide all the body needs." That concept was in the Lord's mind when He forbade us to worry about material things. Notice that the Lord gave a commandment here, as much a commandment from God as the commandments of Moses. While we take scrupulous care to keep from violating one of the commandments of Moses, we seem to have no hesitancy in violating the commandment of the Lord Jesus, who said, "Don't worry about these material things." We do worry about them, and we become enslaved to them.

To prevent that enslavement to anxiety about material things, our Lord, in Matthew 6:25-34, gave reasons why we should not allow material things to become an obsession with us. In the first place, our Lord asked, "Is not the life more than meat, and the body than raiment" (v. 25). What He asked is, "Is man just a body, or is man more than a body?" If man were just a body, the principle thing in life would be to take care of that body. The most important things in life would be what the body eats and drinks, what this body wears, and how the body is to be sheltered. But if man is more than a body, then there is more to life than what a man eats and drinks.

Back in the record of creation (Gen 1) we discover that, after God had made the body, He breathed into it a living soul, and man lived. Man did not live when his body was created out of the dust of the ground; man lived only when God breathed life into him and made him a living soul. What our Lord said was that there is much more to life than what we eat or drink. Because life is more than a physical body and the accumulation of material things, why do we give way to anxious care, rather than trust?

We had nothing to do with creation. That was a work of God. We had nothing to do with the breathing of life into a vessel of clay. That was the work of God. We had nothing to do with new life in Christ, received from God as His gift. That is God's work. The One who created us and the One who made us new creatures in Christ will not surrender His interest in us nor His care over us; therefore, our Lord could say, "Take no thought [do not have anxious care] concerning your life."

In the second place, the Lord pointed to the birds of the air. "Behold the fowls of the air: for they sow not, neither do they reap, nor gather into barns; yet your heavenly Father feedeth them. Are ye not much better than they?" (Mt 6:26). He called attention to God's care of what He has created. When God created, He assumed a responsibility to provide for His creatures. There is no creature that God created that He has abandoned. Even the sparrows are provided for by their Creator. And the God who created us assumed a responsibility to provide for us. We can trust Him to be faithful to His obligation.

By taking anxious care (v. 27) concerning our material needs, we cannot lengthen our days, because God has apportioned our time.

A man may begin with prudent foresight to provide for the future, and the Word of God certainly does not forbid such. Many soon go beyond prudent foresight, however, and make money an end in itself and it soon becomes the god they serve. The Lord did not forbid wise provision for days ahead, but He forbade us to trust what we accumulate as though it could lengthen our allotted span of life. A man may shorten his days by worrying, but he certainly cannot lengthen his days.

In the third place, our Lord demonstrated God's care displayed in nature. "Why take ye thought for raiment? Consider the lilies of the field, how they grow; they toil not, neither do they spin: and yet I say unto you, That even Solomon in all his glory was not arrayed like one of these. Wherefore, if God so clothe the grass of the field, which to day is, and to morrow is cast into the oven, shall he not much more clothe you, O ye of little faith?" (vv. 28-30).

The flower of the field blossoms to display its beauty for a few hours, and then is gone. The flower is temporary, yet God provides for it in creation. If God provides for the temporary, will He not provide for the eternal? God gave you life, and promises to sustain you through length of days. When God brought you into His family as a new creature, He gave you eternal life. God obligated Himself to sustain you throughout the duration of your eternal life. If God will not abandon the lily of the field even though it endures for a few hours, will He abandon those who will dwell with Him forever?

In the fourth place, the Lord showed anxiety is unbecoming a child of God. "After all these things do the Gentiles seek" (v. 32). The love of material things characterizes the heathen. The man without God desires to accumulate because possessions are the only security he has. He has no god to provide for him, no god in whom he can trust. Therefore, it seems wise for a heathen to accumulate all he can. The Lord said that when you make the pursuit of material things the goal of your life and find security in material things, you put yourself on the level of a heathen who has no god. But that which may be fitting for a heathen is unfitting for a child of God.

Then, "Seek ye first the kingdom of God, and his righteousness; and all these things shall be added unto you" (v.

33). What the Lord said is that the center of life for the child of God is never to be material things. The center is not things but a Person. The life of a child of God is not to be corrupted by riches. "Seek ye first the kingdom of God, and his righteousness." "That in all things he [Jesus Christ] might have the preeminence" (Col 1:18). When a child of God makes the pursuit of material things the goal of his life, to the point of being enslaved by them, his life is off-center. What has come to have preeminence in his life has no preeminence in the mind of God. A child of God should make it the goal of his life to seek God's righteousness, not material things.

Finally, the Lord pointed out that worry about the future and material things is pointless because God gives us one day at a time. "Take therefore no thought for the morrow" (v. 34). He did not forbid us to make plans, but He said we do not need tomorrow's food today. Therefore we do not need enough reserve to buy tomorrow's food and pay tomorrow's rent and next month's obligations today, because God gives us one day at a time. "The morrow shall take thought for the things of itself. Sufficient unto the day is the evil thereof." Men measure riches by how much we have today for many days ahead. That is not a biblical viewpoint. The life of faith does not trust God to give today what we will need for the rest of our lives. The life of faith trusts God to give today what we need *today*. If we have all we need today, we are rich.

Now, when our Lord gave these seven reasons why we should be preoccupied not with material things but with the Kingdom of God and His righteousness, He drew a conclusion: "Therefore [since these seven reasons are true] take no thought [do not give way to anxiety], saying, What shall we eat? or, What shall we drink? or, Wherewithal shall we be clothed? . . . for your heavenly Father knoweth that ye have need of all these things" (vv. 31-32). You are your Father's child, and He assumes an obligation to take care of not only your soul but also your body. He asks you to trust, rather than to worry. God's antidote to worry, anxiety, love of material things, is very simple

—trust a faithful God. God has yet to fail His children. Therefore, do not be so enslaved to material things that their love produces anxious care in your life. Rather, trust the loving Father to do what He said He would do. "My God shall supply all your need according to his riches in glory by Christ Jesus" (Phil 4:19).

You cannot serve the wrong master and experience the peace of God in your life. When you pursue the righteousness of Christ, and trust Him to work out His perfect will in you, you are delivered from slavery to things and from worry over them. May God give us such a confidence in Him that we will trust Him and not worry.

22

The Law of Judging

Matthew 7:1-6

God's standard of conduct for His children is His own unalterable, intrinsic righteousness and holiness. Peter stated this so clearly in 1 Peter 1:15-16: "As he which hath called you is holy, so be ye holy in all manner of conversation; because it is written, Be ye holy; for I am holy." When a man asks himself, "How good must I be?" the biblical answer is, "As good as God." While that standard is written into the hearts of all, they acknowledge they cannot attain it. So men universally set aside God's standards and substitute their own. Every religion, no matter how depraved it may be, has its own standards of conduct. But the standard of conduct is not the standard of the character of God, nor of the Word of God.

Paul wrote in Romans 1 that when men set aside the knowledge of God and the demands He makes of them, they make idols like birds, and beasts, and reptiles, and creeping things. Man never sets his own standards above himself, for then he cannot attain the standard he has set. He adopts the standard of something below himself for it is one he can meet. When men legislate godliness and spirituality, they set up man-made laws. They say that if a man obeys these laws he is good, righteous, and he pleases God. Such was the thinking of the Pharisees. They had the standards of the Word clearly before them. Yet, realizing they could not attain the standards of the holiness of God, they set those standards aside and made their own, as they codified biblical standards into a system of rules. They codified the law into 365 negative commandments and 250 positive commandments, and then told men that if they lived by these prohibitions and commandments they would please God.

When a man sets up his own standards of conduct in lieu of the standards of God, he must become a judge of men's conduct. When men make their own rules, they then become judges to determine what is acceptable and what is not acceptable, and to distinguish who conforms to their standards and who does not. The peril of legalism is that it will not lead a man to holiness in his conduct. Also, inevitably, it makes a man judge both the actions and the motives of other men. Because of that, the Lord, in teaching God's standard of righteousness in the Sermon on the Mount, said, "Judge not" (Mt 7:1), Do not become critical. Do not give way to a censorious spirit. What our Lord forbade, because it was contrary to the standards of God's righteousness, needs to be emphasized in our day. "Judge not, that ye be not judged."

The Word of God does not forbid men to distinguish between good and evil. The prohibition, "Judge not," does not give us the right to condone or excuse sin. Paul made this very clear in 1 Corinthians 5, where he referred to a problem of grievous immorality which had come into the Corinthian church. He condemned the Corinthians because they had not removed the one who was involved in the evil. It was a responsibility to safeguard the church against immoral practices, and the Corinthians had been derelict in their duty when they had not removed the immoral man from their midst.

God's Word also makes it very clear that men have a responsibility to discern between the truth and error in doctrine (1 Jn 4:1). The prohibition, "Judge not," does not mean we can pass over false doctrine being promulgated. The Lord said, "By their fruits ye shall know them" (Mt 7:20). What is contrary to the character and the holiness of God is self-evident and is exposed as sin by the Word of God. The Christian must not condone what is openly contrary to the standards of the Word of God.

When the Lord said, "Judge not," He dealt more with motives than with actions. Actions are clear and evident when tested by the standards of the Word of God. But men cannot discern motives and penetrate to the mind and the heart to know another's thinking. That is an area which only God can penetrate, and it is God's right to judge.

Matthew 7:1-6 gives several reasons why the child of God should not have a censorious spirit or sit in judgment upon a fellow believer. The first reason is inferred in, "Judge not, that ye be not judged" (v. 1). What He was emphasizing is the self-evident truth that God is the Judge of men and has not committed judgment into men's hands. Judgment, according to John 5, has been committed by the Father into the hands of the Son, and into His alone. Christ alone has a right to sit as Judge of the thoughts and intents of men. When an individual puts himself in the place of a judge, he usurps God's prerogative; he takes a place that belongs to God alone, and brazenly assumes a responsibility God has not surrendered.

This is very clear in Romans 14:4: "Who are thou that judgest another man's servant? to his own master he standeth or falleth. Yea, he shall be holden up: for God is able to make him to stand." Paul in this parallel passage said no individual has a right to sit in judgment upon another, because God is Judge, and He has reserved that right to Himself.

Again, in 1 Corinthians 4:4-5, Paul affirmed the same truth: "I know nothing by myself [I, by myself, do not have the ability to correctly interpret the motives of my heart]; yet am I not hereby justified: but He that judgeth me is the Lord. Therefore judge nothing before the time, until the Lord come, who both will bring to light the hidden things of darkness, and will make manifest the counsels of the hearts: and then shall every man have praise of God." Men can deal with externals but not with that which is locked up in the heart. But God can penetrate the depths of the thought of the mind and affection of the heart and can correctly determine the motive. When a man judges by externals, he cannot discern what moved a man in his action. Therefore, God, lest men be judged by externals, has reserved the right to judge men Himself, for He can penetrate into the recesses of the person. So the Lord said, "Judge not."

Further, Paul stated that one who judges a brother sins against love (Ro 14:10). And Peter wrote, "Charity shall cover the multitude of sins" (1 Pe 4:8). One judges to expose. When a believer sits in judgment on another believer, he is not judging to cover up but to build himself up in comparison with another individual. Therefore, lest we sin against a brother, the Lord said, "Judge not."

A second reason why we should not judge is, "With what judgment ye judge, ye shall be judged: and with what measure ye mete, it shall be measured to you again" (Mt 7:2). The Lord was dealing with the problem of a double standard. The Pharisees legislated righteousness. They codified the Old Testament into a series of commands and prohibitions which they rigorously applied to others, while exempting themselves. They tested other men by their laws, but exempted themselves from being tested; thus, they had a double standard of righteousness. The Pharisee reasoned, "You are condemned if you do something, because I judge you by that law, but I do not judge myself by that law; therefore I am not condemned if I do the same thing."

If I may paraphrase verse 2, this truth would be clarified: "With the same standard, or by the same standard of judgment that you judge others, you yourself shall be judged; and the same measuring stick that you use to measure others will be applied to you, and you will be measured by it." Our Lord counteracted the idea that what is wrong for one may be right for another— "It is wrong if you do something, but it is all right if I do it." Such a double standard of conduct is contrary to the holiness of God. The standard of God's holiness is applied to all men indiscriminately. Our Lord needed to teach these Pharisees, and those who followed their system, that the same standard of absolute, holy, righteous requirements will be applied to all men.

When one is maliciously critical of another, he criticizes the other to build himself up. He uses the weakness, or failure, or sin of another to promote himself. We fail to realize God does not have two standards, one for us and one for everybody else. But the same standard we use to criticize someone else is the standard by which God measures us; the meter stick by which we measure our brother in Christ is the measuring stick God applies to us. We are tested by the same test we apply to others, and not by a lesser standard; therefore, do not judge.

Verses 3-5 give us the third reason why we are forbidden to judge. This reason may simply be stated: we do not have enough discernment of the true nature of things to be able to judge. Our Lord said, "Why beholdest thou the mote that is in thy brother's eye, but considerest not the beam that is in thine own eye? Or how wilt thou say to thy brother, Let me pull out the mote out of thine eye; and, behold, a beam is in thine own eye? Thou hypocrite, first cast out the beam out of thine own eye; and then shalt thou see clearly to cast out the mote out of thy brother's eye."

The word "beam" signifies a large, hewn timber used in the structure of a building. The man behind that timber cannot see; he cannot determine the true nature of things. In other words, he is blinded. The "mote" about which our Lord spoke is a little splinter, or twig. The man who hides behind the beam so that he is blinded is trying to see a little splinter in someone else's eye. The fact is that both the twig and the beam would blind. You cannot see any more with a little twig in your eye than you can if you are behind a large beam. What our Lord was saying is that man is blind. He cannot see, he cannot determine the true nature of things, yet he puts himself in the position of a judge. He wishes to remove the cause of blindness from somebody else when he himself is blind. How foolish! Our Lord said, when you put yourself in the position of a judge, you are like a blind surgeon trying to remove a splinter in someone else's eye. It cannot be done.

What our Lord was teaching is that man can look only on the external appearance; therefore, he cannot judge the motives of another's mind and heart. When he judges by externals, he does not deal with the true nature of things.

Therefore our Lord said, "Since you in your blindness do not have the ability to determine the true nature of things, do not judge."

Notice the relationship between the beam and the mote—the mote is a little piece of the beam. The Lord indicated that we become most critical of that in others which is a major problem in ourselves. We criticize others for our own weaknesses and see in others most quickly what the Spirit of God condemns in us. What we do when we are critical is to divert attention from what the Lord sees in us to somebody else. The Pharisees condemned men for ungodliness because they were ungodly.

The passage closes with a warning in Matthew 7:6: "Give not that which is holy unto the dogs, neither cast ye your pearls before swine, lest they trample them under their feet, and turn again and rend you." This is the safeguard against looseness or abuse of God's grace. Because our Lord has commanded, "Do not judge," does not mean we can excuse sin. The church at Corinth was faced with a well-known practice of immorality. They had become indifferent to it, and they excused it. Therefore the whole congregation was defiled. They were presuming on the grace of God. Their laxity caused them to take what is holy and cast it to unclean scavengers. When our Lord said, "Do not judge," He did not want us to infer that we should excuse evil, or be indifferent to it as though we had no responsibility. He warned that if we do not condemn what the Word of God condemns, we pervert the truth of God and His grace.

The epistles of the New Testament, in which the apostles warned about the conduct of the child of God, devote more attention to the problems created by the tongue than anything else. New Testament warnings against division are invariably related to backbiting and a censorious spirit manifesting itself in deprecatory words. We do well to heed the Lord's admonition, "Do not criticize, do not sit as a judge upon another man's motives, do not attempt to interpret the desires of his heart." We do not have the ability to discern. That ability belongs to God.

23

Praying with Persistence

Matthew 7:7-12

The Lord taught that righteousness manifests itself in prayer. Prayer is perhaps the greatest manifestation of faith a child of God can demonstrate. In praying we address words to a God we cannot see but we believe exists. We are one among multitudes who are praying, yet we believe God singles out our petition and hears it specifically. We believe God is not alienated from His creation and is able to move in answer to our prayers. The very act of praying is based upon faith. "Without faith it is impossible to please him: for he that cometh to God must believe that he is, and that he is a rewarder of them that diligently seek him" (Heb 11:6).

When a man approaches God in prayer, he must approach with a settled conviction that he believes God actually lives. It would be foolish to address prayer to God if God is so removed from His creatures that He cannot move in their lives. A man must believe that God rewards them that seek Him. It would be utter foolishness to address prayer to God if we were convinced He could not hear.

After the priests of Baal had built their altar and put their bullock upon it, they prayed to their god to ignite the sacrifice and consume it in demonstration that he was god. They "called on the name of Baal from morning even until noon, saying, O, Baal, hear us. But there was no voice, nor any that answered" (1 Ki 18:26). Why not? Because Baal did not exist. Daylong prayer to a nonexistent god cannot and will not bring a reply. God must exist if prayer is to be effective.

Then "they leaped upon the altar which they had made. And it came to pass at noon, that Elijah mocked them, and said, Cry aloud: for he is a god; either he is talking, or he is pursuing, or he is in journey, or peradventure he sleepeth, and must be awaked" (vv. 26-27). Their concept was that their god did not answer because he was too busy with other things. To attract his attention and divert him, "They cried aloud, and cut themselves after their manner with knives and lancets, till the blood gushed out upon them" (v. 28). This went on from morning till night. "There was no voice, nor any to answer, nor any that regarded." Faith in a nonexistent god brings no answer. Faith in a god too preoccupied with his own affairs to be interrupted brings no answer. A god who cannot hear will not bring an answer. The god who is so distant from this universe that he cannot move in it will provide no answers. The one who prays must believe that God exists, and that He is able to hear our prayer as though we were the only one who existed on the earth. God must be so near that His help is immediately available. Faith is foundational to prayer.

But there is an evidence of faith. It is obvious you cannot see another's faith nor can he see your faith, but faith does prove itself. The proof of faith is persistence. If I have a need and tell it to God once, I manifest faith; but you have no evidence of my faith. The evidence of my faith is that I pray again and again, persistently, with patient endurance, until I receive what I ask; until God makes His answer very clear, even though the answer may be negative. Faith produces a patient endurance.

The writer to the Hebrews made this very clear: "Cast not away therefore your confidence, which has great recompense of reward. For ye have need of patience, that, after ye have done the will of God, ye might receive the promise" (Heb 10:35-36). The thought in the word "confidence" is patient endurance. The writer conditioned receiving the promise upon persistence. The hope of the persistent will be realized, if their prayer is in God's will.

"For yet a little while, and he that shall come will come, and will not tarry. Now the just shall live by faith: but if any man draw back [i.e., does not exercise patient endurance], my soul shall have no pleasure in him" (Heb 10:37-38). This makes it clear that God sees patient endurance as the evidence of the genuineness of a man's faith. To ask once may be an evidence of faith, but to persist in petition when the answer does not come is evidence of the genuineness of faith.

The same thought is taught in Hebrews 10:19-23: "Having therefore, brethren, boldness to enter into the holiest by the blood of Jesus, by a new and living way, which he has consecrated for us, through the veil, that is to say, his flesh; and having an high priest over the house of God, let us draw near with a true heart in full assurance of faith." On what basis do we come? First, a way has been opened for us to come by the blood of Christ. Second, we have a high priest who is our intermediary, the Lord Jesus Christ, and therefore we can come. But how are we to come? "Let us hold fast the profession [confession] of our faith without wavering; (for he is faithful that promised)." *Let us hold fast the confession of our faith.* The phrase "hold fast" has in it the idea of patient endurance. A way has been opened by the blood of Christ. We have a High Priest who intercedes for us; therefore, let us patiently endure in faith.

The Lord emphasized this great fact in Matthew 7:7-8. These verses literally read: "Keep on asking, and it shall be given you; keep on seeking, and ye shall find; keep on knocking, and it shall be opened unto you. For everyone that keeps on asking receives; and he that keeps on seeking finds; and to him that keeps on knocking, it shall be opened." A man who prays even once manifests faith; but the man who patiently endures in his praying gives evidence to God and man of the genuineness of his faith. Our Lord said this persistent prayer is a demonstration of righteousness.

James said, "The effectual fervent prayer of a righteous man availeth much [in its working]" (Ja 5:16). The Lord,

in the parable in Luke 11:5-8, showed the result of the
prayer of a righteous man:

> And he said unto them, Which of you shall have a friend,
> and shall go to him at midnight, and say unto him, Friend,
> lend me three loaves; for a friend of mine in his journey is
> come to me, and I have nothing to set before him? And he
> [the one who can meet the need] from within shall answer
> [the intermediary] and say, Trouble me not: the door is now
> shut, and my children are with me in bed; I cannot rise and
> give thee. I say unto you, Though he will not rise and give
> him, because he is his friend, yet because of his importun-
> ity [literally, persistent asking] he will rise and give him as
> many as he needeth.

When the man was at first rebuffed, he did not return home
empty-handed. He persisted until the man gave him the
loaves so he in turn could give them to the needy friend.
Our Lord was not suggesting that God is unwilling to give.
What He was saying is that God oftentimes tests a man's
faith to see if it is genuine and will patiently persist.

Every delay in prayer is a test of a man's righteousness.
Will he give up? Will he become discouraged? Or will he
persist in prayer? Prayer that ceases before the need is met
is not prayer offered in faith. The evidence of the genuineness of faith is that it persists.

Why will God answer the prayer of a righteous man, the
prayer of a man who has demonstrated through persistence that his faith is genuine? Jesus said that it is a father's
nature to meet the needs of his children (Mt 7:9-11). Paul
taught, "If any provide not for his own, and specially for
those of his own house, he hath denied the faith, and is
worse than an infidel" (1 Ti 5:8). It is a father's responsibility, as well as an expression of a true father's heart, to meet
the needs of his chidren. God is our Father. We by faith in
Jesus Christ are His sons, and He will meet our needs.

"What man is there of you, whom if his son ask bread,
will he give him a stone? Or if he ask a fish, will he give
him a serpent?" (Mt 7:9-10). Bread and fish were the two
staples of the Galilean diet. So the child is portrayed as
asking his father for the simple needs of life. When the son

asks his father, the father will not ignore or deceive him. If a sinful man will respond to the petition for the daily needs of his child, will not your Father in heaven meet your needs? "If ye then, being evil, know how to give good gifts unto your children, how much more shall your Father which is in heaven give good things to them that ask him?" (v. 11).

Few have difficulty turning to God in prayer in life's big emergencies. The doctor tells you that you need surgery, and it is not hard for you to pray. Some sudden financial reverse comes, and it is not hard to pray. Some great decision that affects the course of your business must be made, and it is not hard to pray. You recognize that you need others to pray with you, and you call on the saints to join you. But the Lord said that calling on God or joining with the saints in prayer in life's emergencies is not proof that a man is righteous.

The proof of righteousness is that a man calls on God in the little things. The son in theLord's illustration asked his father for a noon meal. The child of God can transform his life by making Jesus Christ a partner in the little things of the day. Pray over the humdrum, the routine, and make Him a partner. When you go to the office and do what you have done a thousand times over, you can escape boredom by making Jesus Christ a partner. This will transform the mundane into something satisfying.

When our Lord said, "Keep on asking," He was not only talking about the crises of life, He was also talking about the little things in life. Paul had this same thought when he wrote, "Pray without ceasing" (1 Th 5:17). To pray without ceasing means to pray about everything. No matter what you are doing, take it to the Lord in prayer. When we pray, we intercede for the crisis. How little praying there is about the ordinary matters! Do you want to be righteous? Do you want to realize and demonstrate the righteousness acceptable to God? Then listen to what our Lord said: "Keep on praying." Make Christ a partner in every detail of life.

24

Living by the Golden Rule

Matthew 7:12-20

Every sermon should have a summation, a conclusion, and an application. In Matthew 7:12-29 the Lord summarized His message, and applied it to the experience of His hearers.

The Pharisees, to make the claims of righteousness attainable, had perverted the Law's original intent. God demanded a righteousness of the heart that would manifest itself in outward acts of righteousness. The Pharisees had ignored the demands of a holy God concerning internal righteousness and had redefined righteousness in terms of a set of external standards. The Son of God repudiated that concept of righteousness, for if acts do not come from a righteous heart, they are not righteous in the sight of a holy God. As the Lord moved through the Sermon on the Mount, He rejected the Pharisaic interpretation and practice of the Law. As He concluded His message, He summarized all He had said about the matter of righteousness in these most familiar words, "Therefore all things whatsoever ye would that men should do to you, do ye even so to them: for this is the law and the prophets" (Mt 7:12).

Matthew 22:35-38 records the visit of a lawyer who came to ask Christ a question. A lawyer in the New Testament was one who was an authority on matters of the Mosaic Law. He was not concerned so much with civil affairs as with religious affairs. He had schooled himself to interpret the fine points of the Law. This lawyer tested Jesus with, "Master, which is the great commandment in the Law?" (v. 36).

For centuries the scholars of the Mosaic Law had wres-

178

tled with problems of the Law. They had tried to condense it to an irreducible minimum. They had concluded the 365 prohibitions and 250 commandments could not be further reduced. Often one law seemed to conflict with another. So the question arose as to which law was to take precedence. If there is a conflict so that you must break one law, which one are you to break?

This lawyer came to Christ, not for information, but to show that Christ was not a wise teacher, that He could not answer the problems inherent in the Pharisaic interpretation of the Law. He asked Him which of the commandments and prohibitions He would put in the place of preeminence. Without a moment's hesitation Jesus replied, "Thou shalt love the Lord thy God with all thy heart, and with all thy soul, and with all thy mind. This is the first and great commandment" (vv. 37-38). A man's love for God takes precedence over everything else. What a man does in fulfilling the requirements of the Law must spring from his love for God. For if a man has a consuming passion for God, the burden of the Law will be light. Then our Lord continued, "The second is like unto it, Thou shalt love thy neighbor as thyself. On these two commandments hang all the law and the prophets" (vv. 39-40).

The Law made demands upon a man's life as far as his social contacts and his responsibility toward men was concerned, for the Law governed not only man's relationship to God but also his relationship to men. Righteousness concerns itself not only with a man's response to God but his response to men as well. As the grievous burdens of the Law were made light by love for God, so love for one's fellow man would make the social obligations of the Law bearable. Our Lord told this lawyer that, if one were consumed with a love for God and love for his brother, there would be no burden or conflict in the Law, for he would do what love demanded. While the Pharisees might see conflict in Law, there could be no conflict in love. Therefore, love would solve the conflict the Pharisees had imagined in the Law.

The background against which Christ spoke to this

Pharisee is in Leviticus 19:18, "Thou shalt love thy neighbor as thyself: I am the LORD." The chapter is concerned with practical righteousness, or the outworking of righteousness, in the life of one who professes to know God and be in fellowship with Him.

First of all, God demands holiness in the life of those who would fellowship with Him. "Ye shall be holy: for I the LORD your God am holy" (Lev 19:2).

Then follow the requirements holiness makes upon the conduct of God's people. They were to honor their parents. "Ye shall fear every man his mother, and his father" (v. 3). "Fear" means respect for authority; it entails submission. Submission to parents was the beginning of the fulfillment of the righteousness of the Law. Why? Because righteousness is the result of submission to God. If a child from infancy does not learn submission to parental authority, when he grows older, he will not submit to the authority of God. So righteousness in adult life begins with learning the principle of submission to the authority of parents. When He describes righteousness, He says children are to fear their mother and their father.

Further, God said, a man shall "keep my sabbaths" (v. 3). The observance of the weekly Sabbath was a sign of submission to God. But a person would not learn submission to God when he was old enough to keep the Sabbath if he had not first learned submission to his parents. He added, "Turn ye not to idols" (v. 4). They were to keep from idolatry. They were to offer their sacrifices to God (v. 5). They were to provide for the poor (vv. 9-10). They were not to reap the corners of their field but were to leave some so the poor could glean. They were also to leave grapes in their vineyard for the poor. They were not to steal nor were they to lie (v. 11). They were not to rob the laborers of his wages (v. 12). They were not to curse nor put a stumbling block before the blind (v. 14). They were not to act unjustly; their judgment was to be a righteous judgment without respect of persons (v. 15). They were not to gossip (v. 16). They were not to hate (v. 17), nor were they to bear a grudge (v. 18).

As one reads through this chapter and sees what God demands, he might feel that God's demands are too heavy to be borne, that the Law is a grievous burden, that there were so many prohibitions that no man could live under such a system. Then comes verse 18: "Thou shalt love thy neighbor as thyself." The Law seems to be an unbearable burden, for there are so many prohibitions no man could fulfill them. Yet if one is motivated by love for his neighbor or for his brother, his burden becomes bearable, because love will not permit him to injure the object of his affection.

Paul used this same principle in Romans 13:8-10:

> Owe no man anything, but to love one another: for he that loveth another hath fulfilled the law. For this, Thou shalt not commit adultery, Thou shalt not kill, Thou shalt not steal, Thou shalt not bear false witness, Thou shalt not covet [a summary of the second table of the Law, governing responsibility to other men]; and if there be any other commandment, it is briefly comprehended in this saying, namely, Thou shalt love thy neighbour as thyself. Love worketh no ill to his neighbour: therefore love is the fulfilling of the law.

How could Paul say, "Love worketh no ill to his neighbour?" The highest love the natural man knows is love for himself. Because of love for himself there is written in his heart a law of self-preservation; the man resists what would be destructive to him and seeks what will benefit him. Paul said that, if I am motivated by the same concern for the welfare of others that I have for my own welfare, I will never do them wrong. "Love worketh no ill to his neighbour"; therefore, love makes the burden of the Law both possible and bearable.

That principle, so clearly enunciated in Leviticus 19, and repeated by Paul in Romans 13, was expressed by our Lord in Matthew 7:12: "All things whatsoever ye would that men should do to you, do ye even so to them: for this is [makes possible the fulfillment of] the law and the prophets."

The rabbis who interpreted the Old Testament stated

this principle negatively. One of the precepts of the rabbis was: "Do that to no man that thou hatest." One could refrain from something injurious to another man, but that would not fulfill the righteousness of the Law; for the Law did not only forbid one to do what was injurious; it commanded that he do what was for his good. The negative interpretation of the rabbis fell short of the righteousness of the Law, for the Pharisees said if you do not pick up a stone and smite your brother, you have fulfilled the Law. If you do not gossip about your brother, you have fulfilled the Law. If you do not steal your brother's wife, you have fulfilled the Law. The brother might starve to death, but as long as you did not injure him, you fulfilled the Law.

Our Lord by His interpretation, summary, and application (v. 12) showed that righteousness is not only to refrain from what is forbidden, but also to do what is righteous. "Whatsoever ye would that men should do to you, do ye even so to them," for this positive righteousness is a manifestation of the righteousness of the Law.

Christ made impossibly high demands in Matthew 5, 6, and 7, and in this conclusion He showed how a man can fulfill the demands of God's righteousness. When a man loves God with a pure heart fervently, it is not a burden to serve Him; it is a joy and delight. The requirements God puts upon a man are not grievous unless love grows cold. If that happens, suddenly what was a delight becomes a burden. God's requirements are not grievous unless there is no love.

What do men want from other men? More than anything else, men look for love, for acceptance, for respect. Men need to be accepted, to be loved, to be needed, to be wanted. One of the problems we face in our society today is that we are all becoming faceless. We are not individuals; we are numbers. Many of our young people in universities rebel because they are not individuals with a personal relationship to a teacher; they are computer numbers. They put their computer number on an examination, and that examination is fed into a computer which records the grade in the professor's office. Young people rebel against this. Why? Because men need to be respected, received, and loved as persons.

If that is what I want, I ought to recognize that is what other individuals want. When my life is governed by this recognition, others' needs will be met, and I will fulfill all righteousness. My concern for another should be patterned after what I care about and am concerned about for myself. Give me what you want for yourself, and you will fulfill the righteousness of the Law.

First John 2:7 says, "Brethren, I write no new commandment unto you, but an old commandment which ye had from the beginning." The commandment that recurs throughout the epistle of John is, "Love one another." Where did John get that commandment? He was in the upper room when our Lord said, "By this shall all men know that ye are my disciples, if ye have love one to another" (Jn 13:35). "This is my commandment, that ye love one another, as I have loved you" (Jn 15:12).

The obligation to love others in order to please God and fulfill the righteousness of the Law did not begin in the upper room. It is as old as the opening chapters of the Old Testament. Consider Leviticus 19: "Thou shalt love thy neighbor as thyself." That is why John said he was not introducing an entirely new concept when he said, "Love one another." He was writing the old commandment. Under the Law, no one could fulfill the Law apart from love, for love made it possible to discharge the obligation of the Law. One cannot satisfy the demands of a holy, righteous God today unless he is motivated by such a love for God that service for Him is a delight, and by love for his neighbor so that obligation for the neighbor takes precedent over his own desires. We may have a tendency to relegate to another age our Lord's demand, "Whatsoever ye would that men should do to you, do ye even so to them." But it is the requirement God places upon His children. Apart from love there can be no righteousness, and without righteousness we cannot please God.

How do I want to be treated? *That* should become my standard of conduct in relationship to others.

25

One Way

A man who hears the truth that salvation is through the Lord Jesus Christ is forced to make a decision. He decides either to accept Christ or reject Him. One who receives Christ receives eternal life; one who rejects Christ is under judgment. As the Lord came to the conclusion of His message to the multitude pressing upon Him, He demanded a decision: "Enter ye in at the strait gate: for wide is the gate, and broad is the way, that leadeth to destruction, and many there be that go in thereat: because strait is the gate, and narrow is the way, which leadeth unto life, and few there be that find it" (Mt 7:13-14).

His hearers were faced with a decision between two radically different ways. One was the way of God, the other the way of man. One was the way of life, the other the way of death. Since the giving of the Law in the Old Testament, Israel had been concerned with matters of righteousness. The Law made it clear that God expected men to be holy, for He is holy; unless a man is holy as God is holy, he cannot come into God's presence. But men were unable to attain to the standards of God's holiness. The religious leaders in Israel, recognizing they did not conform to the demands of the Law, had fabricated a religion which they hoped would satisfy God and be accepted by Him.

Men are born with a conviction of their responsibility to God and know that before they can be accepted by God they must satisfy Him. When men find no way within themselves to please God, they make a way which they

183

hope God will accept. The Lord dealt with the method the Pharisees had devised to please God. Setting aside the absolute standards of the holiness of God, they had accepted man-made standards. As shepherds of sheep they had persuaded the sheep that, if they followed them, they would be led into the fold of God.

The Lord had made it very clear that the righteousness of the Pharisees would never bring the people into fellowship with God (Mt 5:20). This was a crushing blow to the Pharisees and to those who had trusted Pharisaic righteousness to make them acceptable to God.

After the Lord dismissed the righteousness of the Pharisees, He explained why He repudiated it. Pharisaic interpretation of the Law was wrong, for the Pharisees had concluded the only thing that mattered to God was what a man did; if a man behaved himself outwardly, he was acceptable to God even though his heart was unclean. Jesus dismissed the Pharisee's practice of the Law, for, if one does not understand the holiness of God and its demands, he will never conform to those standards in his conduct. Perverting the demands of the holiness of God, the Pharisees countenanced all manner of false practice and yet deemed themselves righteous. Our Lord refers to this, man's religion, as the "broad way."

Because man recognizes he is responsible to God and God must be satisfied because of man's unrighteousness, he sets aside God's revelation, because it is too difficult to attain, and substitutes a religion of his own. But certain things always characterize a man-made religion. Man's religion never imposes demands upon a man that the man cannot meet. It never sets a higher standard for a man than he can attain.

Paul made this clear in Romans 1:21-22: "When they knew God, they glorified him not as God, neither were thankful; but became vain in their imaginations, and their foolish heart was darkened. Professing themselves to be wise, they became fools." In their foolishness, they thought to improve on divine revelation and devise a system which would bring them into fellowship with God.

It seemed to them an improvement on what God had revealed. They devised a religious system and "changed the glory of the uncorruptible God into an image made like to corruptible man, and to birds, and fourfooted beasts, and creeping things" (v. 23). They refused to impose upon themselves standards above those of animals which they could attain, lest they be condemned.

Our Lord warned against the "broad way," the way of man's religion that came as a result of the perversion of divine revelation. Jesus offered instead what He called the "strait gate," or the "narrow way." The narrow way rejects the concept of man's inherent righteousness. It rejects any idea that a man can do something to win favor with God. The narrow way sees Jesus Christ as the only way to life and acceptability with God. This narrow way sees the restrictions that the holiness of God puts upon a man not as limitations but as protection against sin and evil.

Our Lord repudiated what He called "the broad way," and said the only way to acceptance with God was Himself. He made this very clear throughout His ministry. "I am the way, the truth, and the life: no man cometh unto the Father, but by me" (Jn 14:6). Or, as it might literally read, "I and no other am the way, I and no other am the truth, I and no other am the life." There was an exclusiveness in His claims which set aside every other teaching that claimed to be a way to God.

In John 6, the Lord taught this same truth. Following the great miracle of the feeding of the five thousand He taught the multitudes truths about the bread of heaven, the bread of life:

> I am that bread of life. Your fathers did eat manna in the wilderness, and are dead. This is the bread which cometh down from heaven, that a man may eat thereof, and not die. I am the living bread which came down from heaven: if any man eat of this bread, he shall live for ever: and the bread that I will give is my flesh, which I will give for the life of the world. The Jews therefore strove among themselves, saying, How can this man give us his flesh to eat? Then Jesus said unto them, Verily, verily, I say unto you, Except

> ye eat the flesh of the Son of man, and drink his blood, ye
> have no life in you. Whoso eateth my flesh, and drinketh
> my blood, hath eternal life; and I will raise him up at the
> last day. For my flesh is meat indeed, and my blood is drink
> indeed. He that eateth my flesh, and drinketh my blood,
> dwelleth in me, and I in him. . . . Many therefore of his
> disciples when they heard this, said, This is an hard say-
> ing; who can hear it? . . . From that time many of his
> disciples went back, and walked no more with him (Jn
> 6:48-56, 60, 66).

The Lord made it very clear there was no other way to
the Father, no other way to obtain eternal life, than
through Him. One must appropriate Him to have life. Had
our Lord offered Himself as an alternative way, there
would have been little conflict with the Pharisees. Had He
acknowledged there are two ways, the way of the
Pharisees and His way, there would have been little conflict. But when the Lord claimed to be the exclusive way,
the wrath of the Pharisees poured out on Him. Men may be
willing to admit He is *a* saviour, but it is difficult for them
to admit He is *the* Saviour. It was what our Lord demanded.

He made the same claim again in John 10:7-9: "Verily,
verily, I say unto you, I am the door of the sheep. All that
ever came before me were thieves and robbers: but the
sheep did not hear them. I am [and no other] the door: by
me if any man enter in, he shall be saved; and shall go in
and out, and find pasture." The Pharisees claimed to be
shepherds of the flock; the people of the nation were the
sheep. The Pharisees said they would lead the sheep into
green pastures and bring them finally into the fold. But the
Lord said those who claimed to be shepherds were false
shepherds; they were hirelings, not shepherds, and they
would not bring the sheep into the safety of the fold. He
said, "I [and I alone] am the good shepherd." Only as a
man follows Him will he come to life and be brought into
the fold of God. Once again the animosity of the Pharisees
came against Him because Jesus Christ claimed to be the
exclusive way of life. He did not offer Himself as a parallel

way, an alternative way, another way. He offered Himself to the nation as the *only* way.

Peter and John grasped this, for when the lame man had been healed, Peter declared, "There is none other name under heaven given among men, whereby we must be saved" (Ac 4:12). The Lord had this truth in mind when, in the face of those who taught men could follow a man-made system and come into God's presence, He said, "Enter ye in at the strait [narrow] gate: for wide is the gate, and broad is the way, that leadeth to destruction, and many there be which go in thereat: because strait [narrow] is the gate, and narrow is the way, which leadeth unto life, and few there be that find it" (Mt 7:13-14).

The decision about these two ways is of utmost importance because of the destiny involved. It affects not only the course of a man's life but also his eternal destiny. The man who approaches God through the wrong gate ends in destruction. "Destruction," as used by our Lord in Matthew 7:13, refers to complete separation from God. But the man who makes the right decision and enters the right way enters into an abundance of life here and for eternity.

While this truth may be familiar to you, may we emphasize it again. A holy God has the right to determine the basis upon which sinners come into His presence. God has determined that no man can find forgiveness of sins and be accepted of Him unless he receives Jesus Christ as his own Saviour and trusts Him alone for salvation. To offer God anything other than the death of Jesus Christ as the basis of salvation is to offer a man-made religion. It is a "broad way," no matter what form it takes, that leads men eventually to destruction. One must approach God through the gate He has opened. That gate is His crucified Son, the Lord Jesus Christ. "Enter ye in at that narrow gate."

A phone call came to my home while I was away from the city. A four-year-old girl in our congregation wanted to talk to me, but left no word as to why. When I came to church the following Sunday, this little girl came running down the hall. She said, "I wanted to tell you that this week I asked the Lord Jesus Christ to be my Saviour." I said, "Where does the Lord Jesus live now?" She replied, "Right here in my heart." I said, "How do you know?" She said, "Because I asked Him to."

This is a truth so simple a four-year-old can make the decision and know its significance. My heart rejoiced to have this little one come to share with me the decision she had made. A little one can enter in, but she had to come His way. Have you entered in or are you still offering God something which you hope He will accept, but will eventually lead you to destruction? "Enter ye in at the narrow gate."

26

How to Identify a False Prophet

Matthew 7:15-23

Scripture frequently refers to God's children as sheep; those who belong to God are called His flock. Sheep need shepherds. One reason is that sheep are among the most unintelligent creatures God has created. A cow will come home, but never a sheep. Sheep seem bent on wandering and would starve to death if a shepherd did not lead them to pasture. They would die of thirst if a shepherd did not take them to springs to drink. Perhaps that is why God has likened us to sheep. We are not independent. We are not self-sufficient. We cannot get along without a shepherd. If that is true of God's children, how much more is it true of those who have never become the flock of God, who never have turned to the One who could say of Himself, "I am the good shepherd" (Jn 10:11).

Men are hopelessly lost, alienated from God. By themselves they cannot find spiritual food and drink of the wells of salvation. They need one to lead them to the water of life and to the bread of heaven. Because this is true, God from the earliest record in the Old Testament sent prophets to men. Prophets were shepherds. The function of their office was to receive truth from God and communicate it to men so that men might feed on that word. The prophets were in truth shepherds who led sheep into green pasture and beside the still water.

Multitudes pressed upon the Lord Jesus to hear a word from Him concerning the way of life. The Lord Jesus had come as Israel's King, and in fulfillment of the prophecies

189

of the Old Testament He would establish a Kingdom over which He would rule. He invited men to come into His Kingdom. But men could not find the way. The message had gone out that a King was present and a Kingdom was offered, but they did not know the way to find it. The Pharisees considered themselves God's shepherds. They were the interpreters of Moses' Law, self-appointed, but they claimed the authority of Moses. They claimed to be God's spokesmen, but they pointed men to a way that could never lead them to God.

Dissatisfaction with their shepherds and the way their shepherds had pointed them brought this multitude to the Lord Jesus Christ as they sought an answer to the questions, How can a man be made right with God? How can a man be accepted by God? How can one become a part of Messiah's family and His Kingdom?

In Matthew 7:15-20, the Lord sounded a stern warning: "Beware of false prophets." This multitude was viewed as sheep who needed a shepherd; if the sheep were to enter into Messiah's Kingdom, they had to follow the right shepherd; they had to come in the way Messiah dictates, and they need a guide to find it. If they gave attention to the shepherds in Israel, the Pharisaic religious leaders, they would miss the way. They would never come into Messiah's Kingdom.

The true prophet was a voice for God to show men God's truth and to lead them in God's way. The false prophet professed to be a spokesman for God, but he delivered another message. He professed to lead men in paths of God, but led them away from God. They were false shepherds who claimed to be God's voices, but did not speak the truth of God nor lead men in the way of God.

The Old Testament prophets warned Israel about the danger of false shepherds. God said,

> I will raise up a shepherd in the land, which shall not visit those that be cut off, neither shall seek the young one, nor heal that that is broken, nor feed that that standeth still: but he shall eat the flesh of the fat, and tear their claws in pieces. Woe to the idol shepherd that leaveth the flock! the

sword shall be upon his arm, and upon his right eye: his
arm shall be clean dried up, and his right eye shall be
utterly darkened (Zec 11:16-17).

The prophet predicted Israel would come under the rule
of what God calls an "idol" or false shepherd. The false
shepherd would not visit "those that be cut off," the sheep
who had wandered from the flock and were away from the
shepherd's protective care. This false shepherd would not
go out into the byways to seek the straying sheep. He
would leave them there to die. The idol shepherd would
not seek "the young," the little lambs pitifully bleating
because they had been separated from the mother ewe. The
shepherd would not care, nor be moved by the plaintive
cry of the lost lamb. He would leave it to die and would not
go to search for it. The idol shepherd would not "heal that
which was broken." Frequently the leg of the lamb would
be broken as the animal wandered among the stones on the
hillside. It needed the shepherd's tender care to carry it
along with the flock until it was able to walk again. The
idol shepherd would count ministry to the bruised and the
broken too much trouble, and he would be faithless in his
responsibilities. He would not feed that which "standeth
still." Even when the flock had exhausted all the pasture,
the shepherd would seek the shade of a tree on the hillside,
rather than lead the flock to other hillsides.

Rather than caring for the flock, the false shepherd
would care only for himself. He would fatten the lamb that
he might eat it and enjoy the richness of its flesh but would
have no care for the flock. The prophet pronounced the
judgment of God on the right arm and upon the right eye of
this shepherd. The right arm, in the Old Testament, signifies strength, and the eye signifies wisdom. Since this
shepherd would be operating in his own strength and
power, and according to his own wisdom, God said He
would, in divine judgment, bring the strength and the
wisdom of the false shepherds to nought. Thus Israel had
been warned about false shepherds who would lead the
flock astray.

Jesus Christ presented Himself as the Good Shepherd (Jn

10). He warned Israel about the prevalence of false
teachers who would compete with Him for the flock.
Those that do not enter by the door into the sheepfold, but
climb up some other way, are thieves and robbers (Jn
10:1). The Old Testament had foretold that when the Messiah, the true Shepherd, came to Israel, He would be virgin
born. Those who made no claim to have come in fulfillment of God's prophecy nevertheless claimed the right to
lead Israel. The Lord meant that, if the shepherds did not
come to Israel in the way Isaiah the prophet had predicted,
they were thieves and robbers. They were usurping God's
authority over the flock. The Lord said, "All that ever came
before me are thieves and robbers" (Jn 10:8).

"The thief cometh not, but for to steal, and to kill, and to
destroy" (v. 10). Again, "He that is an hireling, and not the
shepherd, whose own the sheep are not, seeth the wolf
coming, and leaveth the sheep, and fleeth: and the wolf
catcheth them, and scattereth the sheep" (v. 12). In these
strong words of denunciation, the Lord described the religious leaders' attitude toward Israel. They were prophets
with no message. They claimed to be shepherds but had no
pasture in which to lead the sheep, and no water with
which to sustain them. They enriched themselves at the
expense of the flock.

In the Old Testament, *wolf* often refers to that which
destroys. Ezekiel used this figure, speaking of Israel: "Her
princes in the midst thereof are like wolves ravening the
prey, to shed blood, and to destroy souls, to get dishonest
gain. And her prophets have daubed them with untem-
pered morter, seeing vanity, and divining lies unto them,
saying, Thus saith the Lord God, when the LORD hath not
spoken" (Eze 22:27-28). The princes and the prophets
were the two ruling classes in Israel when the prophet
wrote. God likened these leaders in Israel to ravening
wolves who sought to destroy the flock, who made the
flock a prey to enrich themselves, who claimed to present
God's message when they had no message whatsoever
from God.

Against this background, the Lord warned (Mt 7:15),

"Beware of false prophets," religious leaders who profess to lead in the way of God's truth but are prophets for their own honor and enrichment. No false prophet would publicly announce that he does not have God's message and he is delivering a message from the prince of hell. He would profess to be God's spokesman to provide them an easy way to find the water of life, the bread from heaven. When false prophets come in sheep's clothing, they are accepted by the flock, for the flock notices only the wool. Looking no further than the external covering, the sheep are satisfied to accept wolves into their midst. In Israel there were religious leaders, who called themselves God's shepherds, who had destroying hearts and were intent on enriching themselves by feeding on the flock. The Lord frequently spoke of the Pharisees as those who were greedy for both power and material gain. They wanted the power that belonged to God's shepherd, Messiah; they wanted to enrich themselves at the expense of the flock.

It is one thing to be warned of the presence of false shepherds, quite another to detect the false shepherd in the midst of the flock. So, the Lord gave the test by which men could determine whether the religious leaders are true or false shepherds (Mt 7:16-18). The test was very simple—look at the fruit. A man with an evil, rapacious heart could not perform the functions of a shepherd for the flock. A man with a selfish heart would never have a concern for the sheep. A man who is wicked within will never manifest righteousness without. "Ye shall know them by their fruits. Do men gather grapes of thorns, or figs of thistles?" Of course not! Why not? Because the life of the root will always manifest itself by the fruit that is borne. You do not have to dig up a fig tree and look at its root to see it is a fig; you look at the fruit. You do not have to dig up a grapevine to examine the root to see if it is a grape. It is evident what the root is by what the fruit is. "Every good tree bringeth forth good fruit; but a corrupt tree bringeth forth evil fruit. A good tree cannot bring forth evil fruit, neither can a corrupt tree bring forth good fruit" (vv. 17-18).

In denouncing the Pharisees, the Lord revealed their fruit that showed what the root was:

> Then spake Jesus to the multitude and to His disciples saying, The scribes and Pharisees sit in Moses' seat [claim to be authoritative interpreters of the Law]: all therefore whatsoever they bid you observe, that observe and do; but do not ye after their works: for they say, and do not. For they bind heavy burdens and grievous to be borne, and lay them on men's shoulders; but they themselves will not move them with one of their fingers. But all their works they do to be seen of men: they make broad their phylacteries, and enlarge the borders of their garments, and love the uppermost rooms at feasts, and the chief seats in the synagogues, and greetings in the markets, to be called of men, Rabbi, Rabbi [Teacher, Teacher] (Mt 23:1-7).

The Lord was saying, "When the Pharisees read the Mosaic Law, do what they say, but do not pattern your life after what they do. Why? Because their hearts are far from the righteousness of the Law. By their works you will know the corruption of their hearts."

John gave the same principle: "Beloved, believe not every spirit [teacher], but try the spirits whether they are of God: because many false prophets are gone out into the world" (1 Jn 4:1). The true teacher is one who says, "Thus saith the Lord." The false teacher is the one who sets aside the revelation God has given and substitutes the rationalization of his own mind. The believer today has the same responsibility God put to those who listened to Jesus' words: "Beware of false prophets. They come to you in sheep's clothing."

Isaiah gave us the test of a true prophet of God, look "to the law and to the testimony: if they speak not according to this word, it is because there is no light in them" (8:20). The Word of God is the test as to whether a man speaks the truth of God, or falsehood. From a heart that denies the Word of God will come all sorts of evil to demonstrate that his interpretation of the Word is false.

In Matthew 23 we find some of the most scathing words recorded anywhere in the Word of God. He pronounced judgment upon the Pharisees. "Woe unto you, scribes and Pharisees, hypocrites" (23:13). "Woe unto you, scribes and Pharisees, hypocrites" (v. 14). "Woe unto you, scribes and Pharisees, hypocrites" (v. 15). The Lord pronounced judgment upon that generation (v. 36) in keeping with what He had said in Matthew 7:19, "Every tree that bringeth not forth good fruit is hewn down, and cast into the fire."

In the presence of multitudes of false prophets, we need to realize there is only one true Prophet. In a multiplicity of shepherds we need to remember there is only one true Shepherd. "Then said Jesus unto them again, Verily, verily, I say unto you, I am the door of the sheep. . . . I am the door: by me if any man enter in, he shall be saved, and shall go in and out, and find pasture. . . . I am the good shepherd: the good shepherd giveth his life for the sheep. . . . I am the good shepherd, and know my sheep, and am known of mine" (Jn 10:7, 9, 11, 14). Jesus Christ is the only Shepherd, the true Shepherd, the Good Shepherd. He is the Shepherd who knows His sheep. He has appointed many undershepherds, but the authority is not in the undershepherd. The authority is in the Shepherd. It is not the word of the undershepherd, but the word of the Shepherd that is life. The undershepherd is faithful as a shepherd only to the extent that he himself follows the Shepherd and leads the sheep in the Shepherd's path. Multitudes today look to men for guidance, for wisdom, for knowledge, but they follow false shepherds, to the destruction of life.

The judgment of God is upon error and those who propagate it. The responsibility of the child of God is to beware of false teachers. For example, be careful when you turn on your radio. Simply because you hear a religious program does not mean you ought to listen. Much false teaching goes out over the air. Be careful to whom you give your mind, whether in listening to men preach or in reading what they have written, for much false doctrine goes abroad from false prophets who profess to be God's spokesmen. Such can never lead to green pastures and still waters. There is only one Shepherd. Walk with Him. Listen to His voice. Follow closely, for He alone can satisfy your soul.

27

Will Religious Men Go to Heaven?

Matthew 7:21-29

When the Lord Jesus Christ was introduced to Israel by His forerunner, John the Baptist, He was introduced as both Saviour and King. John pointed to Him and said, "Behold the Lamb of God, which taketh away the sin of the world" (Jn 1:29), and said another time, "Repent ye: for the kingdom of heaven is at hand" (Mt 3:2). Jesus Christ was introduced as Saviour and Sovereign. Both of these offices demand complete submission to the authority of the One who is Saviour and King. That is why Jesus Christ is called the Lord Jesus Christ. He is the One who has the right to be obeyed. Until men submit to Him, He will be neither Saviour nor King. He is the Lord Jesus Christ.

In order to establish His authority, and to demonstrate to men He has the right to be the Lord Jesus Christ, He performed many miracles. These miracles were obviously not by human power but by divine authority. The nation had evidence that the One introduced as Saviour and Sovereign was the Lord.

Multitudes that came together and heard His words recognized His word was from God. They saw His miracles and recognized His power was from God. An authoritative word was established by the miracles He performed. Multitudes who assembled to hear Him teach and see Him perform miracles acknowledged He had authority from God. He was the Lord Jesus Christ.

As Messiah, He made certain demands upon those who professed a desire to enter His Kingdom. He had come to

197

rule in peace and righteousness. It was for such a ruler that Israel had waited since Old Testament times, for the prophets had predicted God would send Messiah to redeem them and institute a Kingdom. When the nation heard His words and saw His miracles, they debated whether this One could be God's Promised, the Messiah.

As the Sovereign, He made certain demands upon those who would be in His Kingdom. They must be righteous; He could not accept the unrighteous into His Kingdom. The people pressed on Him to have Him explain just what kind of righteousness He required.

In Matthew 5, 6, and 7, He revealed to them they must have a righteousness from God that comes as a result of faith, a righteousness that exceeds the righteousness of the scribes and Pharisees. No man challenged Him that He did not have authority as Lord to lay down the terms by which men are received into His Kingdom. He set aside Pharisaic interpretation of the Law as being a true interpretation and Pharisaic practice of the Law as being true righteousness. He showed them that the only righteousness acceptable to Him and to His Father was the righteousness which conformed to that revealed in the character of God and available by faith.

As the Lord concluded His message to the multitudes, He sounded a warning in Matthew 7:21-23: "Not everyone that sayeth unto me, Lord, Lord, shall enter into the kingdom of heaven; but he that doeth the will of my Father which is in heaven. Many will say to me in that day, Lord, Lord, have we not prophesied in thy name? and in thy name cast out devils [demons]? and in they name done many wonderful works? And then will I profess unto them, I never knew you: depart from me, ye that work iniquity." The Lord did not address this warning to irreligious men. He addressed it to men obsessed with the mechanics of religion. But He made it very clear that religious men do not go to heaven. Religious men are not accepted on the basis of their religion, into the Kingdom over which Jesus Christ will rule. Not everyone that verbalizes the word "Lord" will be accepted of Him.

Obedience is the sign of a true faith. Jesus Christ made that clear when He said, "Not everyone that saith unto me, Lord, Lord, shall enter into the kingdom of heaven; but he that doeth the will of my Father." If one does not obey the One he calls Lord, his disobedience proves he does not own Him as his Lord. The test of whether Jesus Christ is Lord in a man's life is obedience to the command of the One he calls Lord.

Multitudes who had interpreted the evidence that Christ gave in His words and His works pressed upon Him and said, "This one must be the Lord of whom the prophets spoke." But they turned away from Him and walked in disobedience. Our Lord rejected them. Obedience is always the product of faith, and faith the evidence of salvation. Obedience is the demonstration of saving faith.

These men who verbalized the words, "Lord, Lord," but walked in disobedience probably were religious men. They may well have observed the Law meticulously as it was interpreted by the Pharisees. Many of these had prophesied; that is, preached. They had fulfilled the Old Testament prophetic function of publicly declaring truth God had revealed. Further, they had cast out demons. They had done supernatural feats. Further, in the name of Jesus they had done many wonderful works—they had imitated the miracles Christ Himself had performed (Mt 4:23-25). This would seem to be evidence these men were saved, for how could a man preach, and cast out demons, and perform miracles, and still be lost? Yet Christ says they were.

Satan can give to those under his authority the power to perform miracles and to do great feats so it would seem they get their power from God.

> There was a certain man, called Simon, which beforetime in the same city used sorcery, and bewitched the people of Samaria, giving out that himself was some great one: to whom they all gave heed, from the least to the greatest, saying, This man is the great power of God. And to him they had regard, because that of long time he had bewitched them with sorceries (Ac 8:9-11).

Here was a man who preached and authenticated his preaching by performing miracles, but did it all in the power of Satan. That he was unsaved is certain because it was not until Philip came preaching the things of the Kingdom of God that Simon himself believed. He had done all of these mighty acts and supernatural signs by the power of Satan. This authority was given to Simon to deceive men into thinking Satan was the Lord and had a right to be obeyed.

Those involved in the mechanics of religion in our Lord's day (Mt 7:22) preached, prophesied, cast out demons, and healed those that were sick. But they did it in unbelief, by the power of Satan. Yet they mouthed the name Lord.

Jesus Christ said, "Then I will profess unto them, I never knew you: depart from me, ye that work iniquity." The Lord branded all religious practice not performed in faith as iniquity (v. 23), a strong and a startling statement. Multitudes in unbelief assemble in places of worship and go through the mechanics of religion. Do you think God is pleased that men tip their hats to Him? He calls it all iniquity. Multitudes, by Satan's power, may perform great signs. God calls it iniquity. The only thing acceptable to God is a righteousness that is the product of faith. Genuine faith produces works. Genuine faith produces obedience. Unless there is obedience, there is no evidence of faith.

The Lord taught this same truth in John 6, where the record of the great miracle of feeding of the 5,000 is found. As a result of this miracle, innumerable multitudes pressed on the Lord Jesus Christ, even though He had dismissed them and come across the Sea of Galilee with His disciples to find rest. The multitude outran Him and preceded Him to where He would land. When Jesus saw them, He said,

> Verily, verily, I say unto you, Ye seek me, not because ye saw the miracles, but because ye did eat of the loaves, and were filled. Labour not for the meat which perisheth, but for that meat which endureth unto everlasting life, which the Son of man shall give unto you: for him hath God the

Father sealed. Then said they unto him, What shall we do, that we might work the works of God? Jesus answered and said unto them, This is the work of God, that ye believe on him whom he hath sent (Jn 6:26-29).

The multitude had been satisfied physically by the bread and the fish the Lord provided; they had never been satisfied so easily before. They had been satisfied without laboring for their food, and desired to continue without the necessity of laboring for their daily bread. This was contrary to the Word, for God had said, "In the sweat of thy face shalt thou eat thy bread" (Gen 3:19). They wanted Jesus Christ to set aside what was God's established law and to give them bread without their working. Our Lord said to them, "There is only one way you can do the works of God, and that is to believe on Him whom the Father hath sent."

This same truth is presented in James 2:14-20: "What doth it profit, my brethren, though a man say he hath faith, and have not works? can faith save him?" Can that which calls itself faith, but does not work save a person? The answer is, of course not. "If a brother or sister be naked, and destitute of daily food, and one of you say unto them, Depart in peace, be ye warmed, and filled; notwithstanding ye give them not those things which are needful for the body; what doth it profit?" The answer is, nothing. Your word will not satisfy them. "Even so faith, if it hath not works, is dead, being alone. Yea, a man may say, Thou hast faith, and I have works: shew me thy faith without thy works, and I will shew thee my faith by my works." James is pointing out that the only way one can know the genuineness of faith is to see that which faith produces. "Thou believest that there is one God; thou doest well: the demons also believe, and tremble. But wilt thou know, O vain man, that faith without works is dead [barren, sterile, unproductive]?"

Faith is alive. That which is alive will reproduce itself. If there is no fruit in a man's life, it is an evidence the root is dead; that which calls itself faith and does not produce obedience and the fruits of righteousness is not faith in the sight of God. All religious practice and service that does not spring from obedience to Jesus Christ as Lord is called iniquity and is rejected. Apart from works there can be no assurance of salvation.

A man is not saved by making Christ Lord. He is saved by faith in the One who is the Lord Jesus Christ. But the one who is saved will evidence his submission to the Lord Jesus Christ by the works that a living faith produces.

It is very significant that in our day we see waves of supernatural works done in the name of religion. Multitudes of God's people are deceived into believing that because they see so-called supernatural works, those who do them must be people of God. Such is a delusion of Satan; for, until one submits in obedience to the Lord Jesus Christ, what he does (even though it be some great religious work) is called iniquity.

Until a man submits to the authority of Jesus Christ, what he does in the name of religion is deemed by God as iniquity, not good works. We need to beware lest we be deceived by the works Satan can produce to masquerade one of his own as a child of God. Religion cannot save, and the forms of religion do not demonstrate a man is saved. Proof that a man is saved is if his life evidences submission to the Lord Jesus Christ.

Man's needs will never be met by following empty forms of religion, nor by following false teachers, no matter how religious they appear. Man's needs can be met only through a Person, the Lord Jesus Christ.

28

Founded upon a Rock

Matthew 7:24-27

We have been involved in a building program at our church. After the ground had been leveled for our foundation, large equipment was brought in to drill for the piers for the foundation. I heard the foreman on the job say to the operator of the digging equipment, "Keep digging until you hit blueshale rock." If the building was to be permanent, it had to have a sure foundation. If the building were built on the surface, it would shift, and crack, and be destroyed. "Keep digging until you come to blueshale rock."

Buildings in Manhattan stand tall and secure because they are founded upon the rock under Manhattan Island. A boat without an anchor will drift with the tide; it cannot be kept in place unless it is securely anchored. This principle is no less true in the spiritual realm. If a man does not have an anchor for the soul, or a foundation for life, he cannot stand. He will be swept with the tide and drift aimlessly. With this great truth our Lord concludes the great sermon when He says,

> Whosoever heareth these sayings of mine, and doeth them, I will liken him unto a wise man, who built his house upon a rock: and the rain descended, and the floods came, and the winds blew, and beat upon that house; and it fell not: for it was founded upon a rock. And every one that heareth these sayings of mine, and doeth them not, shall be likened unto a foolish man, who built his house upon the sand: and the rain descended and the floods came, and the winds

blew, and beat upon that house; and it fell: and great was the fall of it (vv. 24-27).

The Lord gave a very severe warning. He had been speaking to the multitudes assembled, who sought an answer to the question as to what kind of righteousness a man needed to be accepted into the kingdom Christ had come to institute. How can a man be acceptable to God? The people for generations had been schooled in the teachings of the Pharisees. They said that if men observed the laws of the Pharisees, performed all the rituals, attended the feasts and offered the sacrifices, observed the 250 positive and 365 negative commandments, they would certainly be acceptable to God. But our Lord, against the concerted teaching of the Pharisees, delivered a startling new word. He taught the multitudes it is not by what a man does he becomes acceptable to God, but rather it is by receiving righteousness from God by faith that makes men acceptable to Him.

Here are two contrary systems of thought, and those who heard Him were forced to make a choice. They could not choose both Pharisaism and the word of Christ. It was an either-or decision, and our Lord warned that it would be easy for them to follow the Pharisees. He had said, "Enter ye in at the strait gate: for wide is the gate, and broad is the way, that leadeth to destruction, and many there be which go in thereat; because strait is the gate, and narrow is the way, which leadeth unto life, and few there be that find it" (Mt 7:13-14). Contrasting His teaching with that of the Pharisees, He had likened Pharisaism to a very broad, inclusive gate through which anyone could slip. Our Lord pictured the way He proposed to them was very narrow, very restrictive.

Now, in concluding His sermon, our Lord compared his listeners to those building a house, and he contrasted the foundations on which they were building.

It is easy to build on sand, for sand can readily be prepared for a building; but to hew through rock to find a secure foundation is indeed difficult. Men are always tempted to take the easy path, to follow the easy way, to disdain the labor involved in founding life for time and eternity upon the Rock.

It was this that our Lord pressed home when He said, "Whosoever heareth these sayings of mine, and doeth them, I will liken him unto a wise man which built his house upon a rock." Notice that our Lord called attention to His *words*: "He that heareth these sayings of mine, and doeth them." The word our Lord delivered was the foundational rock upon which a man could build for time and eternity. The doctrine of the Pharisees was shifting sand, an insecure foundation for life now and life to come.

Our Lord emphasized not only the necessity of hearing His words, but also the obligation to respond positively. "He that heareth these sayings of mine, and *doeth* them" (italics added). This truth the Lord emphasized again and again: to hear and to know is not sufficient. To hear and know the truth that salvation is in Jesus Christ does not save a man. Until one commits himself to the truth and to the Person who spoke it, until one receives Christ as personal Saviour, he does not enter into life. To know is not enough. The mind cannot save a man. There must be the heart response to the knowledge the mind grasps, and one must receive Christ personally and trust Him for salvation.

Our Lord made this same truth evident again in John 5:24: "Verily, verily I say unto you, he that heareth my word, and believeth on him that sent me, hath everlasting life, and shall not come into condemnation [judgment]; but is passed from death unto life." *"He that heareth my word, and believeth."* The Lord made it clear that knowledge is not sufficient to save. There must be the response of faith to the knowledge presented.

There is, however, a connection between hearing the Word and believing. A man cannot believe that of which he is totally ignorant. A man must be presented the facts before he can respond for the salvation of his soul. Romans 10:17 made this same connection clear, "Faith cometh by hearing, and hearing by the word of God." Faith is the positive response to a truth presented. When the Word of

God is declared, it calls for a response. When one responds positively and obediently to the truth presented, he steps from death into life. The Word of God and faith are coupled together in salvation. Our Lord emphasized this when He said, "He that heareth these sayings of mine, and doeth them" is the wise man. For this reason Paul said to the believers, "Let the word of Christ dwell in you richly in all wisdom" (Col 3:16). One is brought to a saving knowledge of Jesus Christ by faith in the Word, and the Word becomes the foundation for life here and hereafter.

In contrast to the permanency of the Word of Christ, the Lord spoke of the transitoriness of the doctrines of men. "Everyone that heareth these sayings of mine, and doeth them not, shall be likened unto a foolish man, which built his house upon the sand." Some in the multitudes who heard the word of Christ and weighed the demands Christ made upon them in order to enter His Kingdom concluded the way was too difficult, too narrow, and turned again to the broad, easy way the Pharisees presented to them. They turned to the way of the Pharisees as a result of the decision to reject the Word of Christ.

The Lord said that if they turned again after they had heard the truth presented to them, they were building for time and eternity on shifting sand. There is no permanence to the word of man. Only the Word of Christ has permanence and can give a sure foundation.

The seriousness of this decision our Lord called them to make is seen in the light of the judgment to come. In His illustration, He said that after the building had been completed, "The rain descended, and the floods came, and the winds blew, and beat upon that house" (vv. 25, 27). There will be a test; there will be a judgment. That built upon the solid rock can stand when the tests come, but, when that built upon the sand is tested, the foundation will be swept away and the whole building destroyed. How many houses, built so beautifully on the cliffs along the Pacific, are doomed to destruction because there is no foundation. When the rains come they take the soil from under the house and it slips to its destruction in the Pacific.

Multitudes of men have heard the Word of Christ and have judged His words too restrictive, and have turned to the words of men, little realizing they are bringing themselves certain doom. John wrote in Revelation 20:11-15:

> I saw a great white throne, and him who sat on it, from whose face the earth and the heaven fled away; and there was found no place for them. And I saw the dead, small and great, stand before God; and the books were opened: and another book was opened, which is the book of life: and the dead were judged out of those things which were written in the books, according to their works. And the sea gave up the dead which were in it; and death and hell delivered up the dead which were in them: and they were judged every man according to their works. And death and hell were cast into the lake of fire. This is the second death. And whosoever was not found written in the book of life was cast into the lake of fire.

The righteous, before this great event, had been brought into glory. They had received their glorified, resurrected body. They were safely in the presence of the Rock upon which they were founded.

John described the coming judgment upon the unsaved. They were resurrected to stand in judgment. The test of their foundation now came. Two sets of books were opened. The first book was the book of life, and it was studied to see if their names were written in it. But not one name of those multitudes assembled was found in the book of life, to deliver them from judgment. Then, the second set of books was opened. The books were the record of their evil deeds. These books were consulted to prove they deserved judgment. They were without life, and because of their works they deserved judgment. Thus, the second-death sentence was passed upon them and they were banished from the presence of God forever to the lake of fire.

They had no foundation upon which to stand, no rock under the feet when the judgment came, because when they heard they had not responded in faith. They had turned to the words of men, which became shifting sand.

The word of Christ is opposed to the word of men. The rock is opposed to sand. Life is opposed to death. These are the alternatives Christ presented.

As the multitudes heard our Lord speak they could not but be astonished at His teaching, for our Lord swept aside the accumulated traditions of men and spoke authoritatively the word of God and demanded that men submit to His word. No rabbi ever initiated any teaching on his own authority. They searched the former rabbis to quote them and give authority to their words. But the Lord spoke on His own authority, because He was the Son of God, and He knew the way of access into the presence of God. He had the right to reveal to men the way of access to God, and He said it is not by works, but by faith.

He is the rock of ages. He is the only foundation, "for other foundation can no man lay than that is laid, which is Jesus Christ" (1 Co 3:11). When one by faith in Him has his feet planted upon that foundation, he can stand the test for time and eternity. "He that heareth my word, and believeth on him that sent me, hath everlasting life, and shall not come into condemnation; but is passed from death unto life" (Jn 5:24).

Scripture Index

211

212

214

216

218

Subject Index

Abraham, 7
Acceptance
  of man by God, 19, 45, 48,
    55-56, 57, 60, 85-92,
    200, 204 *See also*
    Righteousness, needed
    to enter God's Kingdom
  of societal rejects by
    Christ, 46-47
Adultery
  act of, 101 103-104
  God's hatred of, 102-103
  Jesus' interpretation of,
    101-104
  Jesus' mercy towards, 46
Alms giving, 128 130-133
Anger, 94-98
  Christian, 95
  equated with murder,
    94-96
Anxiety, 161-165

Babylonian captivity, 12
Beatitudes, the, 19-77
  compared, 69-70
  foundation of happiness
    and righteousness in,
    20
Believers *See* Christians
Blessing (blessed) *See*
  Happiness

Children, 46
Christians
  appointed as
    peacemakers, 64-68
  convict the world of sin,
    74
  light of the world, 81-84

reasons the world hates,
    71-74
  salt of the earth, 79-81, 84
  should expect
    persecution, 74-75
  spiritual appetite of, 40,
    43-44
Christ Jesus
  authority of, 208
  deals with Pharisaism,
    89-90, 92, 93-95
  fulfills the Law, 85-87
  God's love exemplified by
    death of, 96, 124-125
  Good Shepherd, the, 189,
    191-192, 195
  introduced as the Saviour,
    55, 85-86, 186, 197
  introduced as the
    Sovereign, 197-198
  loss of spiritual hunger
    for, 43-44
  love of, 125
  meekness exemplified by,
    37-38
  mercy illustrated by, 46-47
  ministry of, 5-6
  one way to God, 183,
    185-188
  peacemaker, 63-64, 67-68
  reasons the world hates,
    73-74
  revealed as the promised
    Messiah (Deliverer), 5,
    54-55
  revealed by the Law, 14-15
  Rock, the, 203 204-205,
    207-208

219

220

required for fellowship,
61. *See also*
Righteousness
Holiness of God, 19, 96-98
demands sanctification, 88
in the Law, 87-88
provides a standard,
57-58, 127, 166
Home, responsibility in,
38,67
Honesty, 107-114
Hypocrisy
greed tied in with, 148-
149
meaning in original
language of, 135
of Pharisees, 70, 131,
135-136, 146-147, 148,
149

Jeremiah, 12, 77
Judgment
of man by God, 206-207
of man by man, 167-170

Killing. *See* Murder
Kingdom of God
obedience a test of
membership in the, 14
offered to Israel, 5-6
question of righteousness
sufficient to enter the,
7, 19, 49-51, 55-56,
85-92, 204. *See also*
Righteousness, needed
to enter God's Kingdom
to be prayed for on earth,
139

Law (Mosaic), 7-8,
116-118
Christ's relation to the,
85-87
essential character of the,
87-88
goodness of the, 7-8

greatest commandment of
the, 177-178
Israel's need for the, 9-10
lawful use of the, 15-17
love of neighbor in the,
122-123, 178, 180-181
Pharisees' circumvention
of the, 88-92, 184
purposes of the, 7-15
regulatory aspects of the,
15
right use by believers of
the, 116-120
righteousness demanded
by the, 86-87
why Israel given the,
10-15
Law, purposes of, 115,
116-118
Legalism, Pharisaic,
89,93-95, 166-167, 169,
204. *See also* Pharisees,
externalism of the
Light of the world, 81-84
Lord's Prayer, 138-140
Love
fruit of righteousness,
128-130
fulfills the Law, 180-181,
182
giving alms related to, 130
manifests selflessness,
118-119, 119-120
man's need for, 181-182
natural versus
supernatural, 126-127
Pharisees pervert law of,
123-124, 130-131
your enemies, 121-123,
125-127
Love of God, 29, 48, 49,
95-96, 124-125
for sinners, 96, 124
man's, 125-126, 178
Lust, 103-104, 105